Becoming

Fully

Alive

To Danny & Annie

Love,

J. Matthew Nance

J. Matthew Nance

KDP

ISBN: 9798515164294

To Dave Sulack, Bill Smith, Simeon Park, Roger Newman, Ying Kai, Denman Frazer, Bill Fudge, and Ngoc Ha for showing me what it means to swim *supernaturally* upstream toward what pleases Christ, against the flow of a culture that does *naturally* only whatever pleases self.

To those whom I pray will dare to go beyond being a consumer of what's-in-it-for-me cultural "Churchianity" and die to self, becoming fully alive in Christ.

To Tod Lanier for making this book so much better, and to Cheryl Nance, Bob and Mary Carpenter, James Prather, and Nathan Lanier for your assistance.

5.0 out of 5 stars I am a Jesus follower. This book encouraged, educated & inspired me! Loved it!
Becoming Fully Alive speaks my "lover of Jesus" language. I bought 2 books for my sisters. And my husband will read when I'm finished.

5.0 out of 5 stars Great material to keep you focused!
Becoming Fully Alive truly takes us deep into our hearts and makes us feel assured of our salvation in Christ!
The book is not just helpful for your own personal spiritual benefit but is useful for group sharing in any church community.

5.0 out of 5 stars Excellent book
This is an excellent book- doctrinally sound but written on an easily understandable level. Practical life changing truths in an accessible manner. I recommend *Becoming Fully Alive* to anyone who is searching for more joy, meaning, depth or purpose in their life.

Contents

FOMO

How well do you know your texting acronyms? Can you identify the meaning of the following text shorthand?

LOL

IDK

TBH

IMO

LMK

FOMO

How many of those five did you recognize? Here are the words for which the acronyms stand:

Laugh out loud

I don't know

To be honest

In my opinion

Let me know

Fear of missing out

The "Fear of Missing Out" is a social anxiety stemming from the belief that other people might be having fun somewhere, and you are not there. FOMO is usually created by social media, and is characterized by a desire to stay continually connected with what other people are doing. FOMO is really a fear that you might not be living as fully as other people. This generation longs to not let life pass us by.

Young people, you are not the only ones who fear you may be missing out on really living. Many "mature" adults (as if maturity has anything to do with age) show few signs of life, and know it all too well.

Perhaps you are "mature." You are still in existence. You haven't flat-lined yet, but you have stopped daring, stopped changing, stopped adapting to our rapidly shifting world, and stopped singing and whistling. Rarely does your heart ever race over the possibilities ahead. You instead cling to memories of the way life used to be in *the good ol' days*. But deep down inside you long to become fully alive, to not miss out on what life is supposed to be like.

Whether you are young or old, there *is* a difference between…

… having a heartbeat, and being fully alive

... existing, and zestfully investing self into life

... breathing, and living with exuberance

... posting social media, and engaging in real life

What does it take to become fully alive? What is the difference between existence and real life?

Based on what I see and hear when I am at the gym, the answer to what it means to live would be, "Stay in shape. Be thin and attractive. Stay sexually active. Keep young forever. Keep on top of your physique and your psyche. Do these things, and you will be fully alive." If that were true, then all young, attractive, buff, sexually active people would be on cloud nine, but they are not.

People who work smart and work hard, allowing them the finer things of life might say, "To become fully alive, do exciting things. Go on adventure trips. Fill life with luxury. Accomplish all you can. Be good to yourself." But after bull riding, sky diving, climbing the corporate ladder, and building bigger barns, these same people still feel empty. Something is missing; becoming fully alive doesn't come from gaining the whole world.

Why are we not experiencing a full, meaningful life? Because life does not flow into us through the body. Neither does it come to us through our own effort. *We* cannot produce life. How many of us have ever breathed

10

life into dust and caused it to become a human? Or taken a buried seed and caused it to become a living plant? Or even given a bird a beak? There is only One who creates real life, and He does it way better than us.

God imparts true life into our souls, not our veins. God is delighted when the people to whom He gives physical life turn from self to seek relationship with Him. He created us to be *fully alive*, And He longs to see us flourishing and thriving.

Life comes to us through receiving the Spirit of God, not through human striving. Through dying to self and surrendering all to Christ, we enter into real life in the Spirit. We must become like a seed. In order to burst forth with new life, we must die to self and be buried with Christ. It's only through death to self that real life in Christ springs up from within. Those who die to self-directed living and yield to Christ-directed living come up from among the walking dead, raised with Jesus to a super-naturalized higher life not humanly possible.

For the new spiritual principle

of life "in" Christ

lifts me out of the old vicious circle

of sin and death.

Romans 8:2 (Phillips)

Christ lives within you …

The Spirit gives you life…

Romans 8:10

There is biological existence inside all human skin, but there is real life only for those who are in Christ. You might ask, "What are you really talking about? Isn't this just some religious phraseology that Christians use to try to convert people?" What an intelligent question. Thanks for asking! What *are* some *concrete* differences between the supposed supernatural life of those who have submitted themselves to Christ's control versus the natural experiences of all humans?

Is one difference that normal people don't go to church but religious people do? Or is it that most people walk the beach in their free time but goody-goody people get off the pew, walk the church aisle, and pray with the pastor? Is it that most people dig right in at meal time but holy people make a show of bowing to pray in a restaurant?

Or maybe on Sundays, while the common crowd is swimming at the pool, Jesus freaks feel a compulsion to wash away their sins in a baptistery pool. Perhaps the difference is that normal people spend their disposable income on their own enjoyment while the religious person has scruples about tithing.

Or could it be that, as good as they are, all these actions could be performed by someone who still has not entered into a supernatural, life-giving relationship with the Creator? It may surprise you that nothing we just described brings about super-naturalized living. The original followers of Christ described the supernatural life of those in Christ very differently than it is commonly perceived today.

Every person *physically* born out of the womb does as he or she pleases. Later, there is a vague guilt before God for ignoring the will of the Creator and shame for not thinking of the good of others. In sharp contrast, the person who through faith in Christ is born *spiritually* into a real life of connection with the Creator no longer has that dark cloud of condemnation hovering over him or her (Romans 8:1).

God, You fully accept me!

The natural person who has not entered into life with God through a spiritual re-birth has no sustaining power to overcome stubborn harmful thoughts and actions, while the one who is born anew into God's life has power to overcome even the darkest forces within (Romans 8:2).

God, You free me from sin's power over me.

The person who is in Christ is a peaceful soul instead of a troubled soul (Romans 8:6).

God, Your Spirit controlling my mind gives me peace.

The one given over to Christ is in good with God instead of being at odds with God (Romans 8:10).

God, through your death on the cross I am fully alive!

The natural person only has vague concepts of what God might be like, but the one who has surrendered to Christ knows God intimately as His child (Romans 8:14,16).

God, You adopted me as Your child.

The person with only biological life does the best he can with what he has, just like everybody else. Yet the one who loves the Lord is empowered by God's supernatural Spirit within to live in difficult times above the circumstances, sharing in God's radiant brilliance even during tough times (Romans 8:17).

God, You empower me to soar while suffering.

While the natural human sees death as an inevitable end without a clear view of what if anything might come afterwards, the Christ follower has a certain hope of a perfect, eternal bodily experience free from suffering (Romans 8:21-25).

God, You will bring me into Your glory forever.

Human nature is weak and helpless, but those with God's Spirit within have supernatural assistance to overcome natural weakness (Romans 8:26).

God, Your power overcomes my weaknesses.

Murphy's law takes the day for the person who only has biological life, yet the one submitted to the Lord sees how God works everything out supernaturally in life toward his or her favor. (Romans 8:28).

God, You work out everything in my life for the good.

Human skin only knows human love which may walk away any day, while the super-naturalized person experiences God's awesome inseparable love (Romans 8:31-39).

God, Your love will never leave me!

And these differences are just to name a *few*! There are many more in the pages to come.

Let's sum it all up right here from the start: *What identifies a real Christ follower is a super-naturalized personality.* Such a personality comes from walking daily in the Spirit of God. As the very presence of God Himself, the Spirit comes to live within a person when he or she submits to Christ as the One in charge. The Christ follower has a new mind, a new heart, a new will, a new appetite, and a new energy. Let's explore these exciting truths together in the chapters to come.

Johnny Cash was a very popular country music singer in the 1960s. Then in 1967 his growing fame and fortune resulted in drugs. He was cancelling shows, unable to sing because of his addiction's effects on his voice and mood. Johnny was in and out of jails, hospitals, and car wrecks. He described himself as walking death.

Drugs isolated him from everyone. In October of 1967, Johnny Cash decided there was no hope for him. He went North of Chattanooga, Tennessee into a deep network of caves. Without a flashlight, he crawled as far down into the earth as possible, expecting to slowly die and never be found. Johnny said that his separation from God and from people brought the deepest loneliness he'd ever felt.

Yet there in the cave, God unexpectedly became very real to him. A stirring of hope came to his heart. Instead of wanting to die, Mr. Cash suddenly was desperate to live. Yet from deep down in the earth, how could he ever find his way out? Soon he felt a breeze begin to blow and followed the airstream out. That day, Johnny Cash turned his life over to Christ, giving the Lord complete control.

For the remainder of his life though he still had struggles, he couldn't wait to get up every day and get into God's word as truth leapt into his heart. The Lord turned Johnny's life around from walking death to becoming fully alive.

What identifies a real Christ follower is a super-naturalized personality.

On a scale of 1 (low) to ten (high), how alive do you feel day to day? How might an observer of your life describe your definition of "the good life?" What caught your attention in this initial overview of Romans eight? Are you breathing but not really living fully? What needs to change in the way you are thinking, feeling, relating, and living?

So now the case is closed.

There remains no accusing voice of condemnation

against those who are joined in life-union with Jesus,

the Anointed One.

For the "law" of the Spirit of life

flowing through the anointing of Jesus

has liberated us from the "law" of sin and death.

For God achieved what the law was unable to accomplish,

because the law was limited

by the weakness of human nature.

Yet God sent us his Son in human form

to identify with human weakness.

Clothed with humanity,

God's Son gave his body

to be the sin-offering

so that God could once and for all

condemn the guilt and power of sin.

Romans 8:1-3 TPT

When Your Travel Agent Tries to Send You on a Guilt Trip

Shao Feng grew up in a very remote farming village in East Asia, on land that would barely produce any crops. A strikingly adorable little girl, at age twelve she was told that, for the entire family to have food, she was to go live in the city and work.

Lonely and afraid, Shao Feng began working in a restaurant. It wasn't long until she noticed that the men paid quite a bit of attention to her. With just a bit of flirting, she could have them begging to pick her up after work was done. Shao Feng decided to sell herself to men. She found a group of other teenage girls doing the same.

One day a man "hired" the entire group of girls, only to lock them in a room and tell them they now worked for him. He fed them, brought them clients, and provided housing and clothing. Shao Feng was guilty of a terribly wrong lifestyle, and she knew it. She was daily reminded that she "owed" a debt to those who provided for her new lifestyle, and that debt kept her in bondage. She felt she was condemned to be an outcast forever, with no idea of how long she had to work or how much she owed. She felt doomed to an animalistic existence of slavery.

Then one day, a co-worker told her of some group providing a way of escape, and even protection from those who enslaved her. It seemed too good to be true, but Shao Feng was willing to try anything, even at the risk of her own life. So just as planned, one day as they were out back hand-washing their clothes, a van pulled up. Shao Feng and four other girls hopped in.

Christ followers driving the van took them to a textile factory in a city on the East Coast. It was far enough from where they had been held in captivity.

In the factory, Shao Feng learned the skill of fashion design, and started a real job creating dress patterns for factory production. Shao Feng became a fashion designer.

The Korean factory owners were Christ followers, who had decided to locate their factory in Shao Feng's country because so few people there had heard the good news of real life in Jesus Christ. Since the factory was highly profitable and provided a considerable boost to the country's economy, the communist government authorities simply overlooked the spiritual gatherings inside the factory walls.

Every Sunday morning, hundreds of workers in the factory gathered for the weekly "staff meeting," which began with fervent praise worship. After pouring their hearts out in worship, the workers listened intently, taking notes as they prepared to go into other factories and share the good news there as well. Never before had they heard the truth of God's word, and they soaked it up with hungry souls. A passionate Bible message was given to them each week, often by an American who had gained creative access into the country where missionaries were not, and still are not, allowed.

Shao Feng had never even heard the name Jesus before she came to the factory. As she began to hear and read of God's love for her, she began to have hope that maybe there was a way out of the shame which still imprisoned her. Within a few weeks, she asked the Lord to forgive her of all the sin in her life, believing that Jesus died and rose again to give her new life. Slowly she began to come to life, realizing that for the first time ever there was, even for her, *no condemnation, no bondage, and no debt*! She was finally becoming fully alive!

Guilt is real. There is a reason why you and I feel guilt. We *are* guilty. This generation has been told, "Never feel guilty about anything. Just do whatever may seem right in your own eyes. There *is no* standard of right or wrong to even feel guilty about. I'm OK. You're OK."

This generation needs to know that a sentence of guilt has been justly announced on all mankind by our Creator. All of us have ignored our Creator and have lived self-directed lives. This is called "sin." All of us have sinned and come way short of the Creator's intent. He made us to know and enjoy Him. Yet we don't want to know Him and we can't imagine that He could be enjoyed.

So we condemn ourselves to merely exist while on this earth, missing out on the life God designed for us. Then at death we continue into eternity separated from God and all things good. These are the results of our sin. (Romans 3:23, 6:23)

A person without Christ does not do evil against his or her own will. He does it voluntarily and spontaneously. And for that, he or she is responsible before God.

Sin is a huge problem, producing genuine guilt before God. Only someone who is morally perfect could stand before Holy God and legitimately plead "not guilty." Our sin…

- condemns us before God,
- puts us in powerless bondage to our own self-destructive self-centeredness,
- creates an ever-increasing debt we owe God
- separates us from God now and forever

It is impossible for us to earn our own freedom. We need someone to show up at the back door and

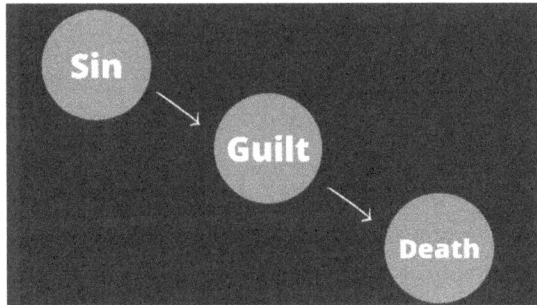

help us escape our own depravity. Where is that rescue van?

Good news! God has provided a way for us to escape from sin, guilt, and death. His perfectly sinless Son has offered to stand before perfect holy God in the place of you and me. He has taken the penalty of our sin instead of us. He died the death of a sinner though He never sinned.

Though His substitutionary death for us has already occurred, we still must choose to turn from self and say yes to His offer of rescue. When we turn to Him, we become forgiven and perfect in our standing before God.

Those who are stubbornly self-reliant somehow insist on simply doing the best possible to live good lives without giving over control to Jesus. While culturally accepting his death and resurrection as historical facts and as church doctrine, the inward being quietly says "No" to allowing Jesus to really be in charge. Choosing to say no to Him results in missing out on becoming really alive.

Are you in Christ? Is Christ in you?

If you are not sure, agree with Him that you are a sinner. Ask Jesus to forgive you through His death on the cross. Ask Him to raise you, through His resurrection power, to new life free of the slavery of sin, guilt, and death. Open your heart and soul, and let God's Spirit come in to reside as Sovereign over you. Jesus is your rescue van.

Even for those who have said yes to Christ and have been fully pardoned of guilt, along comes the damnation squad, reinforcing our guilt, and leading us to believe there really *isn't* a way of escape. The guilt-tripper uses our own mind against us by planting thoughts there designed to destroy our souls. What do you do when travel agent Satan tries to send you on a guilt trip, instead of allowing you into the rescue van?

When your travel agent tries to send you on a guilt trip, say…

"I belong to Jesus! No condemnation!"

So now there is

no condemnation

for those who

22

belong to Christ Jesus.

Romans 8:1

Christianity is the only faith framework that gives a legitimate and adequate solution to the problem of guilt. The solution is for a person to be "in Christ Jesus."

When you turn from self-directed living and surrender your will over to the control of Christ there is new life, free from any condemnation from God whatsoever! You change places with Jesus. Jesus takes on your sin and guilt, and you take Jesus' perfect standing before God. Though you do not become perfect, the Father sees you just as He sees His Own Son Jesus.

As a Christ follower, you still feel the powerful tug of sin, but you have God's Spirit within, which empowers you to worship and walk with the Creator, instead of merely existing by bodily instincts.

Do you belong to Jesus? If so, you have an enemy, and he will try to use the tool of guilt to keep you down. He will try to smother you under the dark, heavy clouds of shame. He may try to guilt-trip you by putting condemning people into your path, or even through messing with your own thoughts. He may point out your imperfections, occasional sinful impulses or brief slips into sinful activity, trying to convince you that you are still condemned by God.

What do you say to the guilt-tripper? "I belong to Jesus! No condemnation!"

The religious leaders brought an adulterer to Jesus to be condemned. Jesus told them to cast stones at her if they were not guilty. After doodling in the sand, He turned to her and said, "Where are your accusers? Does no one condemn you? Neither do I condemn you." Jesus did not come to this world to condemn but to save from sin.

You were rightly declared guilty, and condemned for ignoring your Creator's design for your life and living for self. But if you have placed your life in the hands of Christ, He has removed the guilt, the condemnation, and the shame! Jesus took the sentence placed down on you! God has nothing against you! Jesus was condemned so you don't have to be condemned.

The sin we have within *does* have God-given condemning authority. Yet when we come to Christ for salvation, that condemnation is removed by the higher authority of God's love shown on the cross. When the guilt-tripper tries to send you on a trip, personalize God's promise by putting your own name into His Word. "There is now no more condemnation for _____ because I am in Christ Jesus."

So when the accuser attempts to bring in to your mind condemning thoughts, the Christ follower must take authority. Hang a sign at door of your mind, reading, "No Vacancy!'" Tell the enemy to go away and don't come back another day!

But what if believers sin? There is no "what if" about it. We *will* sin. The Spirit of God within believers' hearts convicts us of our sin, but does not condemn us. There is a loss of *fellowship* with God but there is no loss of *salvation*. We have not practiced our faith perfectly, but our position of right-standing before God has not changed. There is no condemnation for those in Christ. Period.

The difference between the sin of a person who is not in Christ and a believer who sins is the difference between a man who violates the state laws and a husband who has not been kind to his wife. One is found guilty before a judge, while the other has wounded his lover's heart. When a Christ follower sins, it's not a matter of God's condemning judgment, but of a wounded love relationship.

Understand the difference between conviction and condemnation.

Conviction of the Holy Spirit within a believer comes from *grace*, and seeks to bring you to *repentance*.

Though condemnation is the reality of those yet to repent and turn to God, a feeling of condemnation within one who has turned to Christ comes from Satan's own *guilt*, because he himself is condemned and seeking to pull you down into *destruction*.

Satan cannot stand to see a Christ-follower victorious over the guilt and condemnation of sin. Whatever specific guilt he tries to bring your way, own the guilt of that specific sin, but tell the accuser that the blood of Christ has cleansed you of that very guilt and set you free from its condemnation.

The removal of condemnation extends beyond our past sins. When you as a Christ follower sin again, condemnation is not waiting in the wings to return. "No condemnation" means that Jesus exchanged places with you! He took the guilt of all your sin, past, present, and future, and gave you His irrevocable right standing before God.

You are secure in God's favor, forever! If the enemy tries to get you to carry guilt forward, remind yourself that Christ has already carried that sin and guilt to the cross and nailed it there. Get your mind in line with the truth of no condemnation. Get your heart in tune with the freedom of no dark cloud of guilt hanging over you.

Inspectors are required to hang a sign on a dilapidated, dangerous building: "Condemned: Unfit for Use." Just bring the bulldozers and tear this one down. The accuser says, "You are unfit to be a servant of God. Your story is over. You have no more opportunities." The enemy of your soul would hang a "Condemned" sign on your life. Do not Satan hang his sign on you! Refuse to let that guilt-tripper back in to your soul. If you are in Christ Jesus, there is no condemnation.

How does a Christ follower become guilt-free? It's not because you are so perfectly Christ-like! It's because your Savior is so perfectly … Christ! He gives undeserved pardon from sin to those who submit to His Lordship. When your travel agent tries to send you on a guilt-trip, there is something you must say. "I belong to Jesus! No condemnation!" There is a second thing you must also say.

"The Spirit set me free! No bondage!"

"And because you belong to him,

the power of the life-giving Spirit

has freed you from the power

of sin that leads to death."

Romans 8:2

Before you came to Christ, one power was at work within your body; the power of your own flesh, which was very willing to be involved in sin even when you fought it with your best human effort. Fighting sin within by self-effort is as futile as fighting a fire by pouring fuel on it. The more you try to overcome sin in your own power, the more it overpowers you, like a wild animal. Just try adhering to strict, moralistic, man-made rules, and you will soon see that human nature is weak, and is prone to satisfy self instead of God.

When you come to the cross of Christ, exchanging your life with His, Jesus pays your sin debt, and brings within you a new power previously unknown and unavailable. The power of the life-giving Spirit of God within you sets you free from the destructive, deadly power of sin. The Spirit releases you from slavery to sin, and delivers you from the dark master who had control over your life. You have hopped into the rescue van, my friend!

In the 1950s, the people living on the Korean penninsula experienced an invasion by force. The intruding armies captured city after city, pushing all the way to the southern tip of the land. But other forces soon arrived and pushed the invaders half way back up the penninsula to the thirty eighth parallel line. At that demilitarized zone in 1953 stood for a limited period of time a "freedom bridge," where people were allowed to cross over from the north into the south and be free from enemy captivity.

Are you held in bondage by sin's shackles, captive to your own cravings? While there is still time, cross over from self on the throne to Christ on the throne of your heart. The Spirit is your freedom bridge! He has convicted your heart of the reality of your captivity to sin. He has empowered you to turn from sin, and has given you the faith to trust in the finished work of Christ on the cross. Come to Christ. He will cleanse you. Jesus will remove your condemnation. He will set you free from the slavery of sin and the shame sin brings. No more bondage! Jesus is the chain breaker.

The Spirit has done what human effort could never do. Human reasoning says, "Pump harder and you will eventually get water out of God's well on your own." Even still, your life remains a dry desert. The Spirit comes along and provides living water springing up from inside you, gushing out of your life, and refreshing others around you.

Human effort to obtain virtue and merit says, "Row your boat faster and you'll navigate up the mountain stream to where God is, at the top." But the more you row, the farther down the mountain the current pulls you. The Spirit comes along and puts His sail on you, fills the sail with His wind, and lifts you into the air to soar above it all! There seemed to be no way out of sin and no way up to God. Jesus is the way maker.

Imagine me holding a pen. What if I let the pen have it's own way because it wants to be left alone? What would happen? It falls to the ground. What happens when you insist on your own way? Sin pulls you down like the law of gravity.

Now imagine me reaching down and picking up the pin. Gravity is still in effect, but not ruling. Why? The pen does not have life. I do. The Spirit has life and gives life. Life in the Spirit over rules the sin pulling us down to death! The Spirit lifts our lives above the bondage of sin! He roles our heavy load over on to Jesus. Jesus is the burden bearer.

When the guilt-tripper tries to take you on a guilt trip, say, "I belong to Jesus! No condemnation! The Spirit has set me free! No bondage!" There is one more thing you need to say.

"The Father has cleared my charges! No debt!"

The law of Moses was unable to save us

because of the weakness of our sinful nature.

So God did what the law could not do.

He sent his own Son in a body

like the bodies we sinners have.

And in that body he declared an end

to sin's control over us

by giving His son as a sacrifice for our sins.

Romans 8:3

Remember the 1980's chorus?

"He paid a debt He did not owe.
I owed I debt I could not pay.
I needed someone to wash my sins away.
And now I sing a brand new song
Amazing grace the whole day long.
Christ Jesus paid the debt that I could never pay.[1]"

When you are debt free, you are free indeed! If the Son through His death has set you free, you are free to really live!

Those in Christ don't just survive. We thrive! We are supernaturally filled with life. God has cleared every single charge against us, lifting the terrible burden of debt that weighed so heavy on us. The same power that raised Jesus from the dead has invaded our souls and lives in us. His power in us makes us able to be more than conquerors, victorious over sin. We are becoming super-naturalized!

A brother and sister were at Grandma's house for a few days. The boy was shooting his bow and arrow, and accidentally killed one of Grandma's ducks. His sister was watching from the kitchen window and saw him do it. She went outside and whispered to him, "Better do what I say, or I'll tell Grandma."

> Jesus was condemned so you don't have to be.

When Grandma asked the girl to help wash dishes, she said, "It's my brother's turn." The boy ended up a slave to his sister and to the guilt he felt about killing Grandma's duck.

Author unknown[1]

Finally, the next day when his sister said it was his turn to vacuum, he blurted out, "Grandma, I killed your duck." Grandma smiled and said, "I was watching out my window, and saw it all. I have been wondering how long you would take to tell me. I forgive you. Forget it child!"

When you come to God confessing your sin and trusting in Jesus for forgiveness He declares that you are no longer under any dark cloud of guilt.

Do some verbalizing about who you are in Christ.

I belong to Jesus! No condemnation!

The Spirit set me free! No bondage!

The Father has cleared my charges! No debt!

Discussion Questions

1. When you were a student, who had power to influence you to act differently, perhaps without even saying anything to you? Was their influence on you toward the wholesome side, or toward the not-so-wholesome side of life?

2. Read Romans 8:2. What are the two influential powers mentioned, playing tug-of-war within the believer?

According to Romans 8:2, are these two powers equals? Which one has greater influence on the person who has yet to come to faith in Christ?

Which one has greater influence on the Christ follower?

What are the results of belonging to Christ, in light of this power struggle within?
(See also Romans 7:21-25)

3. Read Romans 8:1. To be "in Christ" is to have God's condemnation permanently removed. Condemnation is gone, never to return. If that were not the case, Christ followers who sin would become lost again (condemned again). Christians would always move back and forth between saved, lost, saved again, lost again, ad nausea. No, Christ followers who sin do not get un-adopted by the Father. Even so, sometimes believers struggle unnecessarily with guilt.
Is there something you still hold against yourself? What?

Is there a fear of others condemning you? Why?

As you consider whether you are "acceptable" or not, whose opinion of you matters most?

_____ Your Own?
_____ Other People?
_____ God?

4. Is there someone guilt-tripping you? Who? What will you do about it?

Do you guilt-trip yourself? What needs to change? What new habits can bring God into partnership with you in banishing guilt?

Which of the following results of guilt might others see in you?
_____ having to prove yourself
_____ defensiveness
_____ sensitivity to criticism
_____ serial disposable relationships
_____ lack of joy in prayer
_____ lack of expressiveness in worship
_____ addiction
_____ unworthiness
_____ little sustained motivation to be holy
_____ few resources for self-control
_____ obedience out of fear and duty

Use the truths found in God's word to fight against the enemy as you write a letter …

"Dear Guilt-Tripper, …"

5. Read Romans 8:3. What the law could never do, because your lower, sinful nature robbed it of all potency, God has done by sending Jesus as a substitute payment for your sin debt. What will you do with such amazing grace, freeing you from condemnation, bondage, and debt?

6. Read Romans 8:1-5. Note here the descriptions and roles of the Holy Spirit.

God sent us his Son in human form
to identify with human weakness.
Clothed with humanity, God's Son gave his body
to be the sin-offering so that God could once and for all
condemn the guilt and power of sin.

So now every righteous requirement of the law
can be fulfilled through the Anointed One
living his life in us.
And we are free to live, not according to our flesh,
but by the dynamic power of the Holy Spirit!
Those who are motivated by the flesh only pursue what
benefits themselves. But those who live by the impulses of
the Holy Spirit are motivated to pursue spiritual realities.

For the sense and reason of the flesh is death,
but the mindset controlled by the Spirit finds life and peace.
In fact, the mind-set focused on the flesh fights God's plan
and refuses to submit to his direction, because it cannot!

For no matter how hard they try, God finds no pleasure
with those who are controlled by the flesh. But when the
Spirit of Christ empowers your life, you are not dominated
by the flesh but by the Spirit.

And if you are not joined to the Spirit of the Anointed One,
you are not of him.
Now Christ lives his life in you! And even though your
body may be dead because of the effects of sin, his life-
giving Spirit imparts life to you because you are fully
accepted by God.

Romans 8:3-10 TPT

Profile of a Super-Naturalized Life

On Luzon island in the Philippines, Adolpho lives in a coastal village near Baggio. His village is situated on a water inlet; a perfect place to be involved in the fishing industry. Perfect that is, until typhoon Thelma hit the village. Not only were all the homes wiped out, the inlet's water level increased permanently by over three feet. The land the people owned and loved was now under water, and that water was not going anywhere. The few hundred people of the village scurried inland to dry ground, and huddled together on the dirt road leading down to their village.

Until that day, Adolpho had never sensed that he needed God's help. For that matter, he had never really felt the need for anyone's help; he had not even felt the need to connect with others or with God. Adolpho was a loner. He spent his spare time getting drunk and causing trouble. On that day in 1991 his home and his means of living were suddenly swept away.

As he retreated to higher ground with the people of his village, Adolpho noticed farther up the road a small group of Christ followers praying, and decided to join them in asking for God's help. For the first time ever Adolpho spoke to God out loud. It was as if He believed not only in the existence of God but also in God's ability to hear prayer and respond with care.

The people of the village were exhausted, and slept that night on the road. The next morning, the Christ followers asked everyone to join them in prayer, asking God to show them what to do. After the prayer, one of the believers suggested they go into the bamboo forest and cut bamboo poles. They would use the poles to make new homes on stilts above each family's land, to make walkways from house to house, and to make fish-raising areas between houses. Another believer said that instead of having individual fish farms, the village should work together, creating a fish-farming Co-Op.

Everyone loved these ideas, went right to work, and recreated a village on top of the water above their land. The new village was better than the one they had before. Many people in the village submitted to Christ, and gave the first of every ten fish as an offering at church.

With the fish, the church now serves lunch to the entire village every Sunday. I ate some of those fish, as did the team of students on a mission trip with me from Korea seminary. We were so blessed by seeing God at work among restoring the livelihood of a village. Adolpoho's glow for God is contagious.

The church sells each week's remaining fish to maintain a shuttle bus taking villagers to and from the market. Adolpho drives that bus. The new Adolpho is greeting every person coming on and off the bus. He is enjoying connecting with people and with God as a way of life he never knew before. Getting drunk is far from Adolpho's mind.

When we had the privilege of worshipping among these fine people in their village and staying in their above-water huts for two weeks, we were amazed at their joy, their zest for life, and their love for God and for others. There was no human explanation as to the kind of people they had become through the crisis. The indwelling Spirit of Christ caused Adolpho and many in his village to become fully alive through a devastating set of circumstances. The Spirit super-naturalized their personalities.

What identifies a Christ follower is not a fish bumper sticker or a cross necklace. The Christian is not identified by membership in a religious institution. Nor is he or she automatically a Christ follower by being born into a respected, law-abiding, hard-working family. Not even being a God-fearing person who knows that Jesus died on the cross to forgive sins causes a person to become fully alive with God's Spirit within.

You can know that the fire truck is ready to put out fires yet still never call on the fire department to save your house.

You can know that Jesus died on the cross to forgive sins, and still never call on Christ to take away your self-centered heart and give you His life.

You can know that the resurrected Lord has power to kill the old you that loves sin, and even know that He can empower you to turn away from self-centered sinful living, and yet never allow Him to invade your life.

You can cry at the sight of Jesus suffering on the cross for you and still not turn from sin to give yourself to Christ.

You can believe that there is power in the blood of Jesus to forgive sin and still never ask Jesus to cover you with His forgiveness through His death on the cross.

You can say "Amen" when the preacher says, "you must be born again" and never have done so yourself.

It is possible to be churched all your life, cultured and moral, respected and Christianized without ever having received new life through Christ. You can be culturally "Christian" without ever becoming super-naturalized into real life by the Lord's power.

What is the profile of a real Christ follower? *What identifies the real follower of Christ is a super-naturalized personality.* Such a personality is not a do-it-yourself project. A super-naturalized personality is the *result* of walking daily according to the Spirit of Christ within.

What follows is not the *method* to develop such a personality. Neither is what follows the *means* to achieve godliness. Methods and means point to human effort, which is futile in changing sinful human nature. But when God's Spirit works within a person, the same power Who created you *recreates* you. Here are five *results* of a personality which has been transformed by the life-giving power of the Spirit of God invading the soul of one who dares to let Christ redirect life.

The real Christ follower is someone with…

A Heart Gripped by the Spirit's Promptings,

Not by Human Nature.

God…sent His son…

so that the just requirement of the law

would be satisfied for us,

who no longer follow our sinful nature,

but instead follow the Spirit.

Romans 8:3-4

The natural man's whole existence is limited to the human ability of the flesh; what can be achieved by self-effort, what virtue might be attained through human striving, and what pleasures might be found in this world. The natural man thinks of self as basically good. For the natural person, measuring his or her own moral muscle may become an obsession. Yet that muscle has no endurance to stay consistently strong in good works. It cannot upgrade the depravity of the human soul.

Finally, self gets tired and frustrated. *I can't!* If the Christ life is being lived out by someone nearby, self becomes hopeful. *I think just maybe…Christ can!*

He already has! He died for you on the cross. At the foot of the cross, your heart opens and in comes the Holy Spirit of God Himself, replacing mere *human nature* with God's *super-nature* and His supernatural power. That old former love of self-effort is now dead and buried, having been replaced with an embracing of the Spirit's prompting and power. The super-naturalized person has the power to consistently say "no" to self and say "yes" to God.

As a person *super-naturalized by an invasion of the Spirit* into every part of your life, you become eager to hear from the Spirit within, waiting to be prompted by the Holy Spirit instead of acting on your own impulse or instinct. You have a new heart of love for God. The former love for the world is replaced with a passion for enjoying God. You enjoy being loved by God, loving God, and loving others as Christ loves. When cultivated, the new craving for full, daily surrender to the Spirit within is stronger than fleshly cravings.

Jesus came to transform you into someone with authentic right living flowing out from the fullness of the Holy Spirit within.

He came to offer you the greatest exchange ever. He gave His life so you could live. When you surrender control of your life to Him, His Spirit invades and empowers you to live holy, set apart for God's use.

When Cheryl and I married in 1984, I went to her parents' home with a flatbed truck and a winch. She had worked to buy her own VW Bug at sixteen, but on the first drive she accidentally put it in forward instead of reverse. She rammed it into the brick wall at the end of the driveway. It had set right there rammed into the wall for six years, wrecked and ruined.

With the little bug on the flatbed, I went to Uncle Bert's house. As a VW enthusiast, he took that 1967 wrecked Beetle, which didn't run, and in exchange gave me a 1978 VW Rabbit, which ran and even had AC! Uncle Bert was satisfied and so was I. Was my father-in-law satisfied? Not so much. But he got over it!

Coming to Christ means exchanging your wrecked junk of a life for His bright, beautiful, holy Self supernaturally living in you and through you. It is the greatest exchange ever. Christ takes your death and gives you His life. God is satisfied. You are satisfied. Is the devil satisfied? Not so much. But he *will* get over it.

Following rules can't make you right with God or give you a heart for living right. But when you surrender the control of life over to Christ, your heart becomes gripped by the Spirit's promptings instead of human nature. No more sporadic redoubling of efforts to be virtuous every now and then. Instead, when you die to self and allow the resurrection power of Christ to invade your soul and take charge, the Spirit makes you right with God through Christ's death.

> *The joy of God went through the poverty of the manger as well as the agony of the cross.*
> Dietrich Bonhoeffer

Dietrich Bonhoeffer dared to speak out against Hitler and his anti-Jewish racism, and as a result was put in prison. The natural man would dread the suffering of prison, become bitter, and display rage. Bonhoeffer's reaction was that though his body was in prison, his soul was in Christ, with a sort of joy that outlasts pain and anguish. He said that *the joy of God had gone through the poverty of the manger as well as the agony of the cross. That joy looks death in the eye, and finds life!* Bonhoeffer's heart was gripped by the Spirit's promptings to respond to suffering in a way not humanly possible.

A real Christ follower is someone with a heart gripped by the Spirits' promptings, and with...

A Will that Seeks to Please the Spirit, not Self.

Those who are dominated by the sinful nature

think about sinful things,

but those who are controlled by the Holy Spirit

think about things that please the Spirit.

Romans 8:5

The natural person seeks and relishes things of human origin. It's only ... *natural*. The super-naturalized person seeks and enjoys the things of God.

From the beginning of our physical lives at birth, we trust in our own effort. Such striving leads either to frustration due to weakness or self-deception due to perceived strength, resulting in either pride in self or brokenness.

It's at the point of brokenness that we become willing to turn from self-directed living and *seek help from Someone larger than life.* Turning to the cross of Christ for forgiveness and new life, we are born a second time. This spiritual birth opens an entirely new realm of ultimate reality and gives us access to God's higher perspective. When we experience God's great love in a personal way, the will shifts from seeking what pleases ourselves to

44

seeking what pleases the new Resident within the human heart: the Spirit of God Himself.

Does this describe you? If it does, you are becoming fully alive in the Spirit. Keep following the Spirit's promptings in your heart and mind. Keep giving the Spirit freedom to show you what pleases Him.

If this Spirit-led life does not describe you, come to the cross of Christ, turn from sin and self-centered living, ask Him to forgive you and make you into a new person. He will do just as you have asked, and will begin to redirect your life as you move from self-gratification to God-glorification.

> Move from self-gratification to God-glorification.

Two words in Romans chapter eight verse five describe the contrast of the natural life and the super-naturalized life. Those two words are "flesh" and "Spirit."

The flesh is life by human power. It is living independently of God. Natural human life takes God-given desires and twists them for selfish gain. The need for shelter becomes greed to build bigger and bigger barns. The felt need for physical intimacy becomes sex outside of marriage and pornography. The need for food becomes gluttony and laziness.

Though the flesh often refers to obviously sinful attitudes and actions, even things appearing to be respectable things can be fleshly. Do you have ambition to excel as a professional regardless of the hidden ethical path it takes to get there? Do you strive for excellence in religious service, whether singing or teaching, but do so for your own glory instead of deflecting the glory to God?

These are but two examples of appearing like a godly person while operating in the flesh, not the Spirit.

The flesh strives to gratify self. The natural person tends to think anything that is pleasurable must be acceptable. The fleshly nature of man says anything that brings pride in human effort must be good. Anything that engages ambition must be a worthwhile cause. Such is the natural fleshly nature of humans.

Let's contrast the flesh with the Spirit. The Spirit is like a strong wind. The strength of God's Spirit causes you to move in ways you could not move if left to yourself. The Spirit is like God's breath breathing into you. You receive through the Spirit a higher rate of oxygen in your lungs and are able to climb higher than if you did not have God's breath. The Spirit is a mystery of unseen yet very real supernatural power at work on your human will, changing you in ways the natural man cannot understand. Your very inner nature is changing through the work of the Spirit.

The person who is *born physically* uses the flesh as life's power. If you, however, have come to the cross of Christ to surrender your all to Him, you have been born a second time. You have been *born spiritually*. Before Christ, you were spiritually dead, but now you have come to life. You have a new spiritual life with God and you enjoy the Spirit's powerful wind blowing into your life's sails. You enjoy what the Holy Spirit reveals. You genuinely seek to submit all of your life to whatever pleases the new Spirit within you.

As a super-naturalized person,

Your most frequent thought…

> is Christ.

Your greatest love...

> is Christ.

Your strongest desire…

> is Christ.

Christ: your highest affection.

Christ: the only One you expect to satisfy you.

Christ: your source of confidence.

Christ: your foundation for a healthy sense of self.

Your true personal identity is found only when you enter into a personal relationship with Christ, who supernaturally transforms your personality.

A drunk driver shouldn't drive. He will hurt himself and others. He should give the keys to someone who is sober, and let another person take control of the wheel. That's the only way he gets to where he's supposed to go.

Perhaps you are behind the wheel of your own life, and you shouldn't be. You weave off and on the road. You drop down into the ditch and pop back up into oncoming traffic. You are out of control. God is *ready* to take the keys. Yet you must choose to give Him control. You must let Him take the wheel and be in charge. That's the only way to arrive at the destiny He has planned for your life.

Whether or not you experience a super-naturalized life depends on whether or not you are willing to submit your will to His will. When you do, you will shift from pleasing self to pleasing the Spirit of God. The Spirit stands ready

> Your true identity is found only when you allow an invasion of Christ's Spirit into your core.

now to breathe God's refreshing breath into your weary soul.

The real Christ follower is someone with a heart gripped by the Spirit's promptings, not by human nature, and with a will that seeks to please the Spirit, not self. The real Christ follower is also someone with …

A Mind Preoccupied with the Spirit,

not Instinctive Actions.

So letting your sinful nature control your mind

leads to death.

But letting the Spirit control your mind

leads to life and peace.

Romans 8:6

What do you think about when your brain has no distracting input? When there's no noise, no voices, no demands, and your mind is in neutral with the time and space to roam freely where does it go? What obsesses you? That thing is what you orient your life around, whether you realize it or not. Your life orientation is either killing you or energizing you.

You might say that sometimes you are spiritually minded and other times you are more carnally minded. Though the person who has invited the Spirit to freely invade and take over his life still has the ability to sin, the truly born-again person has a new, over-ruling obsession.

If you have the Spirit-oriented mindset, you are not occasionally interested in the things of the Spirit off and on; your whole being centers on life in the Spirit. Your absorbing interest is pleasing the Spirit. You are delighting in what the Spirit does. Without the Spirit within, you would constantly struggle within to overcome sin. (See Romans 7:14-25.) With the Spirit, you are more than a conqueror.

If your mind is preoccupied with basic instinctive cravings, you fixate on getting rewarded with what you feel you must have. If you get what you crave, you are happy and proud of yourself. If you don't get what you desire, you are frustrated and mad. You obsess over satisfying the demands of the human body. Think about it. Does the human body come out of the factory with a satisfaction-guaranteed warranty? It carries no warranty with it except the certainty that it will one day cease to function. Living to satisfy your body is literally a dead-end effort. Such is life in the flesh.

Life in the Spirit is much different. If your mind is preoccupied with the Spirit, you turn away from the world and open wide your heart to Christ, discovering real life and peace. You give greatest attention to God as He brings you out into a spacious and free life of wellness, wholeness, and integration of all parts of life. While you still have the biological life known to the natural man, you primarily have a supernaturally abundant, zestful life filled with purpose. Such life is *not* known to the natural man.

Either a world orientation is killing you or a God orientation is energizing you. Which way does your life compass point?

The real Christ follower is someone with a heart gripped by the Spirit's prompting, not by human nature, with a will that seeks to please the Spirit not self, with a mind preoccupied with the Spirit not instinctive actions, and with…

An Appetite for Welcoming the Spirit,

Not for Welcoming Sin.

For the sinful nature is always hostile to God.

It never did obey God's laws, and it never will.

That's why those who are still under the control

of their sinful nature can never please God.

But you are not controlled by your sinful nature.

You are controlled by the Spirit

if you have the Spirit of God living in you.

(And remember that those who

do not have the Spirit of Christ

living in them do not belong to him at all.)

Romans 8:7-9

It is natural for you to think that every human being is a mixture of good and evil, and the goal of life is to strive toward doing more good than evil. Surely God will be pleased with such effort, right? Though such a concept may cause you to follow a moral code, it has several serious flaws.

Good and evil are *not* equals. *Evil trumps good in the natural man* because mankind is born in the depravity of sin within; from birth we inherited from the human race a bent toward serving self, instead of serving the One who created us to serve Him. The natural man has a sinful nature, and regardless of the level of good intentions or best efforts, can never please God.

Good trumps evil in the super-naturalized person because the power of the resurrected Christ lives within. The one who has been born again is no longer controlled by sinful nature. You either have the Spirit living in you, and thus have become right with God and are able to overcome sin, or you don't have the Spirit within you and thus you are at odds with God and cannot overcome sin. Which describes you? It's not a mixture of both.

Unless there is *within* you Someone who is *above* you, you will soon give way to whatever is *around* you, and you will be at odds with the One *above* you.

If there is within you Someone who is above you, you will soon rise above the sin around you, and you will crave more and more of the One above you.

An appetite for sin ignores God, and God isn't pleased at being ignored. He created you to enjoy Him, not ignore Him.

An appetite for God ignores sin, and sin isn't pleased at being ignored, but it *will* get over it and so will *you*.

Let God take up full residence within you, and be completely at home in your heart. The Holy Spirit is actively warning against left-over earthly mindedness in the one who is born again.

He will tell you when there's danger in the home of your heart.

When the Spirit dwells within you …

He's your burglar alarm alerting you of something intruding that wants to steal your joy

He's your smoke detector telling you something in your heart stinks

He's your security check-point telling you something dangerous is trying to come toward you.

The real Christ follower is someone with a heart gripped by the Spirit's promptings not by human nature, with a will that seeks to please the Spirit not self, with a mind preoccupied with the Spirit not instinctive actions, with an appetite for welcoming the Spirit not for welcoming sin, and with...

A Life Energized by the Spirit,

Not by Human Striving.

And Christ lives within you,

so even though your body will die because of sin,

the Spirit gives you life,

because you have been made right with God.

Romans 8:10

The natural human life is one lived on self's terms. The super-naturalized life is one lived on God's terms. The natural person lives by self's best effort, while the super-naturalized person has strength and vitality only the Spirit can bring.

It's only natural for people to have an inclination toward self-improvement, yet only those born again have found the secret to a truly changed life; death to self and new life in the Spirit of Christ. All of humanity is pulled down by the gravity of sin, while those surrendered to

Christ enjoy the hot-air balloon ride of being lifted by the Spirit-wind into a super-naturalized personality and perspective unseen by those on earth below. No longer stuck on the ground! Sin's gravitational pull is still in effect, but the Spirit lift is so much stronger! Ready for the ride of your life? Jesus is ready and waiting for you!

Like everyone else, it's only natural if you are merely trying to make the best of life and just taking things as they come. In contrast, the super-naturalized person has the Spirit within, bringing so much more than this world can offer. A whole new world is opened- the realm of the soul communing with Father God.

Except for Enoch and Elijah of the Old Testament, every single human body throughout history has come to the end of life and ceased to function. Every single human heart stops pumping blood and stops taking in and giving out air.

Go on and try to live your best life now. It ends in death. Give it your best human effort, and at the end will come frustration and death. Only Jesus has the power to fill your years on this earth with the vitality you crave, a new holy energy human striving cannot attain. Surrender all to Jesus, and you will start becoming fully alive. To top it off, Jesus will give you a perfect resurrection body with an eternal warranty!

So where do you stand? Are you a natural person, or have you become super-naturalized? It's all or nothing. Have you *merely added Jesus* into your crowded life? That's nothing. Even Satan has done that. It's time to lose everything and add only Christ and what Christ brings. For you, Is He Lord of all, or Lord of all that's left over?

If you are not joined to the Spirit of Christ, you cannot be your true self. Only by joining to the Spirit are you empowered to become the you He created you to be. It's time for an invasion of the Spirit! Once invaded, you will discover your true self becoming fully alive for the first time.

Discussion Questions

1. An invasion might be defined as one entity aggressively entering territory controlled by another entity and establishing new control. An invasion results in a change of rulers. To determine if you have been invaded by the Spirit, ask yourself...

- Who do I follow? (Romans 8:4)
- Who dominates my thoughts? (Romans 8:5)
- Who orients my life compass? (Romans 8:6)
- Who am I becoming? (Romans 8:7-9)
- Who feels at home in my heart? (Romans 8:10)

2. The chapter referred to life in Christ as the "great exchange." Read Romans 8:3-4 in several modern translations, such as The Passion Translation and The Message Paraphrase. How would you describe the great exchange? Why do we each need the exchange? How can the great exchange happen? How can you identify an exchanged life?

3. What might most people say it takes to become fully alive?

4. What might most people say are characteristics that identify a person as a Christian?

How do those things compare to the five identifiers of a super-naturalized life, as outlined in the chapter?

5. The profile of a super-naturalized life is not a list of commands to obey. The profile describes the *results* of a life surrendered to Christ. Read Romans 8:4-10. What evidence of supernatural life might someone see in you?

6. In each of the following pairs, circle either the left or the right, whichever most applies to you:

Relishes in things of human origin	Enjoys the things of God
Fixated on satisfying personal desires	Opens wide the heart to Christ
Intermittently interested in spiritual things	Absorbing interest is pleasing the Spirit
Life on my terms	Life on God's terms
Trying to improve self	Dying daily to self Christ in me - my all in all
Downward pull into basic human nature	Upward Spirit-lift of personality & perspective
Adding Jesus into my crowded life	In me, it's only Christ and what He brings

7. Who do you know that is truly a super-naturalized person? What leads you to think of them?

Now Christ lives his life in you!

And even though your body may be dead

because of the effects of sin,

his life-giving Spirit imparts life to you

because you are fully accepted by God.

Yes, God raised Jesus to life!

And since God's Spirit of Resurrection lives in you,

he will also raise your dying body to life

by the same Spirit that breathes life into you!

So then, beloved ones, the flesh has no claims on us at all,

and we have no further obligation to live in obedience to it.

For when you live controlled by the flesh,

you are about to die.

But if the life of the Spirit puts to death the corrupt ways of

the flesh, we then taste his abundant life.

The mature children of God are those who are moved by

the impulses of the Holy Spirit.

Romans 8:10-14 TPT

Living Spiritually Instead of Physically

For people born into this world, physical birth brings biological existence. Most of us come to a time in our biological life when we realize there is an internal part of us which is not yet fully alive. This part is the soul. We try to fill the soul with life, using whatever methods we fancy. Life is seen as striving to achieve whatever we can through physical, natural means.

Some try to fill the soul by indulging in bodily pleasure or living a life of comfort and luxury. Others seek to satisfy the craving of the soul by becoming the best possible version of self, through achievements of one kind or another. Seeking to feed the soul's craving, we may lunge into family life, sports, hobbies or climbing the professional ladder. Some eventually give up on soul satisfaction and decide instead to escape the pains of reality in some way.

God made our bodies. That is true. But don't be fooled. Your real life is not in your body. The potential to become fully alive is about your soul becoming filled with the only thing that will satisfy it. God created you, and He gave you a soul. He put a longing within your soul to know Him in a personal way.

You can fulfill all the demands of your body and yet, if your soul's hunger for God is not met, you will be restless. Searching for the meaning of life, you may feel empty inside despite great accomplishments. At the end of it all you may be left asking, *Is this all there is?*

Happiness and meaning in life come from the Spirit, not the flesh. When you come to know God personally through Jesus Christ, the Spirit of God invades your soul, and your soul finally finds fulfillment. What are you expecting to bring you fulfillment and meaning? Is your soul still searching in vain, or have you found Christ?

Those who are born a second time have more than biological existence. We are becoming fully alive through the Spirit of God within the soul. The second birth comes when the Spirit of God is invited into the soul. God's Spirit then empowers us to live by God's greater design for us, rather than being powerless over the biological urges within our natural flesh.

> He put a longing within your soul to know Him.

The flesh is driven by ambition, comfort, ego, personal preferences, and the demands of one's self. The only way to battle such dead-end self-centeredness is through the power of the Spirit. The indwelling Spirit is mentioned three times in the two verses we now examine.

If you have received biological existence from your parents, you have physical life from your first birth. If you have made the personal surrender of your spirit to the Spirit of Christ, He has invaded your soul. Now through "Christ in you" (Romans 8:10) you have been given spiritual life. Christ in you satisfies your soul and empowers you to live for spiritual purposes instead of physical purposes.

You have been born a second time into a new spiritual world which you did not know before. You must get to know this new spiritual world, so that you can fully live the life God provides through His Spirit. In one verse you are reminded twice that "the Spirit lives in you (Romans 8:11)." There are three really great motivations and three powerful mandates for living spiritually instead of physically.

Motivations for Living Spiritually

Be motivated to live spiritually instead of physically because...

Sin kills your body.

...Your body will die because of sin...

Romans 8:10

Although sin is alluring, there's a hook inside the lure. Sin looks great, and *is* fun when you bite into it, but then it hooks you and holds you in misery. Sin is bad for your health!

Worry is a sin that causes your hair to fall out. Fear is a sin that causes your jaw to quiver and your teeth to chatter then shatter. The sin of grumpiness turns your face into a prune. Promiscuity causes STDs and lust causes your eyes to bulge right out of their sockets.

Gluttony brings Dunlap's disease, when your belly dun lapped over your belt! Drug abuse kills brain cells. Selfishness causes loneliness, isolation, and sometimes suicide. Greed causes anger, crime, murder, imprisonment, and a living death. Pride, ego, and the desire for power cause dangerous risk-taking, which increases your insurance premiums, which causes marital disputes, which decreases your intimacy as a couple, which... well, you get the idea.

Be motivated to live spiritually instead of physically because…

The Spirit brings your spirit life.

And Christ lives within you,

so even though your body will die because of sin,

the Spirit gives you life,

because you have been made right with God.

Romans 8:10

Sing brings destruction to your body. The Spirit takes all that destruction and starts a restoration project. He takes your brokenness, and puts you back together. Even the scars left by sin are redeemable and useful to God. He takes everything that sin ruined in you and rejuvenates you. All the shame and guilt is removed.

The Spirit comes in to your life and fires your former manager, the sinful flesh. That rascal whipped you with pain. Though the previous manager still hangs around and tries to act like he is in charge, you are now under new management; the invigorating Spirit of God Himself within you!

All this happens when you decide there is nothing you can do within your own fleshly effort to present yourself before God as acceptable. At the end of self, you come to the cross of Christ. You turn from sin, letting the blood of Jesus cleanse you, asking Him to give you new life. You surrender yourself completely to His authority over your daily life. Before the Spirit's invasion, you were a walking zombie. Now you are becoming fully alive and on fire with God's blazing Spirit within you.

Take a poker and put it in the fire. The poker is just *in* the fire. But if you leave it in the fire, *the fire gets in the poker.* The poker becomes red hot! It does not become red hot by stressing or straining. It becomes red hot because of where it hangs out. The fire is hot. The poker is now hot because of being with the fire. The poker now has fire power to set other things on fire.

Christ followers know that the power to become fully alive is *not* in self effort. Christ followers hang out with the fiery Spirit of God and get the Spirit's fire within, gaining the power to set other people on fire for the Lord.

Do you have the Spirit's fire within you? He will motivate you to live spiritually, as His fire burns away impurities of the flesh. The Spirit within causes the soul to find what it has been craving: enjoying the presence of Almighty God Himself. With God's Spirit within, you will find you are becoming fully alive.

Be motivated to live spiritually instead of physically because...

God will bring your dead body alive to Himself!

The Spirit of God, who raised Jesus from the dead,

lives in you.

And just as God raised Christ Jesus from the dead,

he will give life to your mortal bodies

by this same Spirit living within you.

Romans 8:11

The mortality rate of human bodies is so far in history holding incredibly steady right at 100%. One out of every one humans have died or are headed that direction. And those who die not having surrendered to Christ as Lord will be raised from the dead into miserable bodies fit only to suffer in hell separated for eternity from God and all things good.

But those who are possessed by Christ will be raised from the grave and experience the Spirit transforming our decomposed carcasses into super-naturalized bodies able to worship and serve the Lord. The Lord will recompose what sin and death decomposed! We will help reign over the eternal Kingdom. We will never get sick or tired and never grow weary in well doing.

We will have glorified, supra-natural bodies able to somehow transport us from place to place in an eternal city of 1400 cubic miles, and we will never ever need to re-fuel! (Revelation 21:15-17)

God will recreate a new version of you that will be even *more fully and perfectly you than you are now*. Not one ounce of you will end up in the trash bin of the universe, except your sins. They need to be left behind anyway.

Our glorified bodies will never have disease. There will be no sinful urges to fight. No regrets. No shame. Everything this sad life has stolen from us will be fully restored and enjoyed. We will have full energy, full alertness, unmixed joy, full engagement in meaningful activity, and direct access to God, face to face. We get there by grace, God's undeserved favor. Yet we will enjoy differing degrees of rewards, based on the degree to which we lived spiritually while on earth. (Matthew 5,6,25, I Cor. 3)

Let this picture of the believer's future motivate you to live spiritually now: "Our earthly bodies are planted in the ground when we die, but they will be raised to live forever. Our bodies are buried in brokenness, but they will be raised in glory. They are buried in weakness, but they will be raised in strength. They are buried as natural human bodies, but they will be raised as spiritual bodies. For just as there are natural bodies, there are also spiritual bodies." I Corinthians 15:42-44.

May you and I make this our desire: "I want to know Christ, and experience the mighty power that raised him from the dead. I want to suffer with him, sharing in his death, so that one way or another I will experience the resurrection from the dead." (Philippians 3:10-11) We've examined three motivations for living spiritually.

- Sin kills the body, so living physically to please the body is a dead end journey.

- The Spirit brings life, so living spiritually to please Christ in you brings more and more life.

65

- Soon God will bring your dead body alive to Him, so live ready for Him to do so at any time.

In addition to three motivations, there are three mandates from God which direct us in how to live spiritually. So far in our time together in Romans chapter eight, we have looked at how the position and condition of the one who has placed Christ on the throne of life is in contrast to the position and condition of a person whose life still has self on the throne.

Now for the first time in Romans eight we see something beyond *description* of that contrast of the flesh and the Spirit. We now see *directives* given to us, starting in verse twelve. The believer has gained a new *position* of right standing before God, and must begin to *practice* that position; to *work out* in life the holiness which at salvation God has *worked in*.

Mandates for Living Spiritually

Because the Holy Spirit has done so much for you, as a Christ follower you have an obligation to partner with the Spirit in becoming fully alive. Sin kills, so you must kill sin. Here's the first mandate.

When your body talks, don't have listening ears.

Therefore, dear brothers and sisters,

you have no obligation to do

what your sinful nature urges you to do.

Romans 8:12

Who do you have to thank for who you have become? Do you think you owe yourself the good life because of all the sweat equity you have put into your home, your family, your yard, and your career? Are you rather pleased with what you have done by your own effort? If so, then you may have already begun to rationalize dirty little secrets in your life, telling yourself you owe yourself the pleasure. You tell yourself you deserve to have your needs met by your little secret. It's a way of rewarding yourself.

Such stinkin' thinkin' shows you feel an obligation to your flesh; to fulfill your bodily urges because you owe it to yourself. Your sensual nature is great when used within marriage, yet outside marriage, it will easily lead you astray. It will make you think you are obligated to indulge yourself in whatever your body desires.

Your body talks. It tells you what it wants and when it wants it. When your body talks don't listen. Say, "I don't owe you anything, flesh. I've served you too long already, and what a price I paid! But now I've bought into the Jesus life and I don't have any buyer's remorse!"

Everything that you have that's worth anything is something that God has given you through His Spirit. You owe the Lord everything. He has given you His very best. Be loyal to Him, not to your deceiving flesh. Let your heart be drawn to God with gratefulness. Regardless of how far you've come in life, you didn't do it by yourself. The Lord gave it all to you by His undeserved favor. You don't deserve to reward yourself for what *He* has done. You don't owe your flesh anything. Don't listen to your body any more.

Do you think your effort and intelligence got you to where you are today? If so, then you will feel that you owe it to yourself to fulfill your own physical desires. You may follow your self-centered dreams, even if it costs your marriage and your health.

Take that pride you have in yourself and bury it. Get on your way toward really living. The Spirit is calling you to new experiences that will satisfy you far more. The Spirit will surprise you with the power of Christ in you battling *for* you and *with* you in gaining victory over fleshly desires. Tune your ears to what the Spirit is saying instead of the flesh. Now for the second mandate.

Cut the nerve to your instinctive actions by obeying the Spirit.

For if you live by its dictates, you will die.

But if through the power of the Spirit

you put to death the deeds of your sinful nature,

you will live.

Romans 8:13

We ask the wrong questions: "How far can my girlfriend and I go before we cross the line into sin?"

"How many corners can I cut in business and still be following the Lord?"

"How seriously must I apply the Bible? It says, 'Love your neighbor.' My neighbor shot my dog! Love Him? Seriously?"

The right question is, "What do I need to remove from my life to be completely submitted to Christ?" Donald Wyman was clearing trees in a very remote Pennsylvania forest. A tree fell on him and penned his leg. No one was anywhere near. He would die out there, unless he cut off his leg. So he cut it off six inches below his knee, used his belt for a tourniquet, and lived.

Isn't living better than dying? It's time for you, if you are a Christ follower, to obey His command of getting radical about cutting out sin. What sin needs removed? Laziness? Drunkenness? Work-a-holism? Drugs? Pride? Meanness? Worry? Jealousy? Stinginess? Don't aim to slowly wean yourself off such sins. Don't consider which sin you will leave alone for later and which one you will work on now.

Sin.

Must.

Die.

Mortify it. And then get as far away from its stinky carcass as quickly as you can. Don't try to tackle sin in the power of your own human flesh. That's like trying to get rid of termites with a fly swatter. Call on the exterminating Holy Spirit! By obeying the Spirit in little decisions every day, you cut the nerve to your instinctive actions. Ready for the third and final mandate?

Since you are God's child, act like it, by following the Spirit's lead.

For all who are led by the Spirit of God

are children of God.

Romans 8:14

If you have come to Christ for forgiveness and new life, then you have been lifted up to a super-naturalized life! Live like it! You no longer have to fall for the downward pull of sin. You are free to fly! You pilot an airplane now! Always ask, "What seems good to God's Spirit within me?" The Spirit's leading is like the GPS in your plane. As you fly, you don't dare ignore God's Positioning System!

He gives you His GPS, but He does not fly your plane by a remote control in His hand. You must decide what your response will be to the GPS. Will you pull the cables controlling the wing flaps to move your life by God's design, toward the destination He has for you? Or will you navigate on your own without God's Positioning System?

Sometimes there are rats sneaking on your plane trying to chew through those cable controllers! Frederick Handley was a pioneer in early aviation. One day he was doing a solo crossing of the Sahara Desert when he heard a strange sound in the plane. A rat had followed the smell of food into the little plane. Frederick heard it chewing on the control cables in the rear of the plane.

He knew he would die if the rat continued chewing. Yet Frederick had no way to leave the controls to go kill the rat. So he took the plane up to the highest altitude possible. He knew that ol' rat could not survive high altitude. It wasn't long before the sound stopped. When Frederick landed safely at his destination, he checked the back of the plane and found a dead rat right by a control cable partially chewed through.

Are the rats of fleshly desire nipping at you? Climb higher! Let the Spirit take you up to daily quiet time with God. Go to the higher altitude of memorizing and meditating on the Word of God. Soar above sin by fasting. Spiritual disciplines such as these will take you higher and kill the rats of sin, helping you to become fully alive. Ask the Spirit for specific, direct guidance for each and every life situation, and when He gives it, follow Him!

> You've been lifted up to a super-naturalized life! Live like it!

All who are led by God's Spirit are His children. Those who are *not* led by God's Spirit have no assurance whatsoever that they have ever become His child. Who is leading your life? You may profess Christ but does Christ possess you?

Professing that Jesus is Lord is something that even the demons do. Yet they refuse to yield to His Lordship. Many profess Christ, but only those whose hearts are possessed by Him are God's children. It doesn't matter how long you have attended church, how many praise songs you have sung, how much money you have given, or how good your reputation, only by becoming convicted of your true sinful nature and surrendering to Christ can you ever become fully alive.

When you see God as completely holy, you will clearly see your prideful, self-centered heart. It's then that you must confess your sinfulness to God, and ask the Christ who died for you on the cross to forgive you and make you His Child. Ask the Lord to fill your heart with His Spirit and lead you from here to eternity. When you turn from a lifestyle led by sin to a lifestyle led by Christ's Spirit you become God's child.

The fascinating and true book *The Bamboo Cross* tells the stories of how people groups of Vietnam turned from living physically to living spiritually. Sau was a member of the Chil tribe. Like everyone else in his tribe, he grew up believing the spirit of the white python snake must be appeased by blood sacrifice. To please the python, Shamans would lead the people in drunken orgies and the drinking and sprinkling of the blood of a sacrificial water buffalo.

Fear of the python's anger ruled Sau's life. But one day a grandfather came to his village and told Sau of a spirit more powerful than the python, and a blood sacrifice to end all sacrifices. Soon Sau changed his heart allegiance from the python to Christ, and experienced such freedom from fear that his entire village eventually left the python to follow Christ. Drunkenness and orgies were replaced with tribal drums praising the Savior around a cross created from bamboo. Through the witness of the Chil people, other tribes within a day's walk soon turned from living physically to living spiritually.

Discussion Questions

1. Read Romans 8:10. In what ways do you see that sin kills the human body?

2. Read Romans 8:11. Does God's Spirit live in you?

   What did or would a total invasion of the Spirit look like in your life?

3. Read Romans 8:11 and 1 Corinthians 15:42-44. Contrast our earthly bodies with our eternal bodies.

   Most of us struggle in some way with body image. Will we have that struggle forever?

4. Read Philippians 3:10-11, 20-21. Paraphrase these verses in your own words:

5. Of the three motivations for living spiritually, which one most motivates you?

   Which one least motivates you?

6. Read Romans 8:12-14 and review the three mandates for living spiritually.

Have you ever asked, "How far can I go in physical relationship without sinning?"

What's wrong with that question, according to 8:13?

When your body talks to you, expressing its demands, what makes it difficult to ignore?

What makes it easier to ignore your body talk?

What would your life look like if you followed the Spirit's lead in every area?

Which areas might change?

7. Ray Ortlund says, "There is not one ounce of you that will end up in the trash bin of the universe – except your sins, which you want to leave behind anyway." Write your prayerful response here:

The mature children of God are those

who are moved by the impulses of the Holy Spirit.

And you did not receive the "spirit of religious duty,"

leading you back into the fear of

never being good enough.

But you have received the "Spirit of full acceptance,"

enfolding you into the family of God.

And you will never feel orphaned,

for as he rises up within us,

our spirits join him in saying the words of tender affection,

"Beloved Father!"

For the Holy Spirit makes God's fatherhood real to us

as he whispers into our innermost being,

"You are God's beloved child!"

And since we are his true children,

we qualify to share all his treasures,

for indeed, we are heirs of God himself.

And since we are joined to Christ,

we also inherit all that he is and all that he has.

We will experience being co-glorified with him

provided that we accept his sufferings as our own.

Romans 8:14-17

How to Be Sure You Are God's Child

God is pleased when the people He created are fully alive. He is not pleased when our lives resemble a rat race.

When our boys were young, their pet hamster would get on the wheel and run faster and faster, with a very satisfied look on his face like he was really getting somewhere. Then he would get off the wheel to look around the new place where he had arrived. He quickly became confused in discovering he was right where he started. Many of us are like that hamster; giving life the very best we have, but confused as to why we are going nowhere.

Even many who profess faith in Christ are not really living fully alive. Why? At age fifteen, Trevor Bayne had already professed his faith in Christ. But the consuming passion of his life was driving race cars, which led him to move to North Carolina alone at the age of fifteen. Early success in racing as a teenager led to some tough lessons about who was really in control over his career and over his entire life.

At sixteen, he was racing forty-two times a year, when a hummer crash left him injured without any sponsors and without any races. Trevor realized his life was *not* his. God was in charge. His life was not supposed to be about his own talent but about giving glory to God. Yet all Trevor had ever really known about God was what he had read in books. He became tired of reading about God, and decided to give honest prayer a try.

Trevor said, "God I want to personally know you. I want to experience Your power. You are in charge of me. I give myself to you through Christ. It's no longer about me. I'm willing to do whatever You want." That was the day Trevor went from professing Christ to possessing Christ as His Master.

In February of 2011, Trevor Bayne became the first racer to win the Daytona 500 on his first attempt. He was nineteen. Nobody had ever won the race on the first attempt, until Trevor. As big as that is, Trevor says, "The Daytona 500 doesn't define me. Christ defines me. Christ is first. I am second."[2]

For Trevor, and anyone desiring to become fully alive, the real thrill is not living life as if you are on a racetrack. Life's greatest thrill is knowing and glorifying God with all you are. You can visit Trevor and his wife at their coffee shop in Northwest Knoxville, which sells drinks at a racing pace of one every 88 seconds.

A few years ago, I was asked to counsel a couple. They were living together and wanted to understand the benefits of getting married. I got our first session off to a terrible start.

I asked them, "Do you believe in marriage?"

---

[2]iamsecond.com

Instantly they replied in sync, "Of course."

"Will you commit yourselves to marriage?"

Even more quickly and emphatically, they replied together, "No way."

They professed a belief in marriage as an institution good for society, but they would not personally commit to marriage.

Are you sure you are a child of God? Professing Christ is not the same as being possessed by Him! Do you profess belief in Christ as the Savior? Many people in western countries profess Christ to be the Savior but do not possess Christ as their Lord. Have you genuinely become convicted over your sin, asked Him to help you turn from sin and give Him control of your life?

Many have been in church all their lives, but are not certain what God is really like, are unsure of His love, and have only read about Him, prayed what is supposed to be prayed to Him, and sang what is supposed to be sung to Him. They remain secretly unsure of their salvation. That's because many who are *in church* are *not in Christ*. Some leading pastors suggest the number of church members who have not been born again may be as high as forty percent.

Here's a question worth asking. "If I were put on trial today, would there be enough evidence to convict me for being a Christ-follower?" If the answer turns out to be "no," then you have the opportunity to turn from self to Christ. By questioning, you will have avoided the biggest mistake anyone could ever make; missing out on life with God, now and forever. If the answer turns out to be "yes," then you have gained assurance of salvation. Either way, you win, and there is nothing for which to be ashamed.

So the question is, "How can I be sure I am God's child?" You may reply by saying, "Well, I have put my faith in Jesus." Yes, but how do you know your faith is saving faith, not just mental assent to a set of beliefs? We shouldn't put our faith in our faith!

> Many who are in church are *not* in Christ.

Today, may you and I move from man-centered hesitation to God-centered assurance of salvation. The difference between assurance and no assurance is the difference between bobbling like a cork tossed by the waves or moving forward like a confident ship surging through the waves. It's the difference between pushing a perfectly good car without turning on the engine, or hopping in the car to enjoy the powerful engine taking you to your intended destination.

Here are seven descriptions of the person who is God's child. If these describe you, assurance is yours. If these do not describe you, today is the day for *you* to make things right with God by becoming His child.

God's child experiences the Spirit's leading.

For all who are

led by the Spirit of God

are children of God.

Romans 8:14

Are you experiencing inner nudges from God's Spirit within you? The one who is truly surrendered to Christ has God Himself living within. Is God prompting you from within? Is He moving you in directions you would not otherwise have gone? Is there Spirit-led forward movement in your life?

The Christ-life is one of ongoing, spiritual pilgrimage. If your life is static and unchanging, you may not know God. His mercies are new every morning. If you are merely culturally identified with a Christian church, then you likely *resist* change in your life. If you are truly God's child, you *embrace* the change brought on by following the Spirit's leading.

If you have truly yielded control of life over to Christ, then you possess Christ's Spirit within and are changing daily to become more and more like Christ. You are turning from sin in the power of Christ's forgiveness received at the cross. Sin forsaken is an assurance of sin forgiven. So, if you are the way you always have been, you are not a Christ follower. A Christian is a new creation. The old has passed away. Newness comes daily.

Are sins dying and falling off your life in areas such as your thinking, your relating, your scheduling, your financing, and your goal setting? You will know you are saved by the spiritual fruit the Spirit is bearing in your life. If Godly habits, Kingdom generosity, Godly people, and Christ-like thoughts not present before are coming into your life more and more, you are God's child.

Are you closer to God now than you were a few years ago? Are you becoming more and more like Christ in how you love God and love others? If you are born again, you are growing in relationship with God. Maybe a year ago you had trouble knowing how to pray, but now you are talking to God and listening to Him all the time. If you can't talk with God, it's likely a sign you still don't know Him.

When problems arise, do you naturally turn to man-made solutions? Do you turn first to your own solutions? Are you trying to squelch God-shaped needs and instead hoping to fill the void by living up to culture's expectations? You need to surrender your life to the Lord. His child is one who does not follow self's solutions or society's pressure, but is instead led by the wisdom provided by the Spirit.

God's child has left behind God as a distant and dreadful taskmaster.

So you have not received a spirit

that makes you fearful slaves.

Romans 8:15

The Greek word fear is "phobos," from which we get our word "phobia." Do you have a phobia of God? If you don't know God, you *need* to fear Him. Since He created you for Himself, ignoring God is the most fearful thing a person can do.

Those who know Him respect Him immensely, and don't think of Him as "co-pilot" or the "man upstairs."

True believers experience His great love, which casts out fear. What is your mental image of God? Is He somewhere out there? Is He a celestial policeman looking to catch you doing wrong things?

Imagine you are in the sixth grade in the hallway between classes. You are cutting up as usual. Around the corner comes Mr. Principal. He sees what you are doing. You run and hide behind the water fountain. Mr. Principal crouches down and looks right at you with his solemn face looming over you.

Thirty minutes later, that same man goes home, kicks off his shoes, gets on the floor with his kids and his dog, and has a big tickle party. What made the difference? They are his children. You are not.

Do you think of God as Mr. Principal? You are not yet His child. He is not the dreaded slave master you may have in mind. Which of the following describes you?

Slave	Son
Obeys from fear	Obeys from love
Works by threat	Works willingly
Insecure	Secure
Focuses on compliant behavior	Focuses on relationship and attitudes
Has to work without honor	Is honored and invited to work

Do you feel you must do your duty to a higher power or be rejected? Then you may not yet know Him. God's child knows God is not distant and dreadful.

God's child has been adopted into His family circle.

Instead, you received God's Spirit

when he adopted you as his own children.

Romans 8:15

Every human is God's creation. Every single person is created by God in His image. But we are *not* all God's children. Only those who have been adopted by Him through faith in Christ have become His children.

You can legally disown your own naturally born child, but you cannot disown a child you have adopted. Adoption is permanent. When you die to self and commit to live for Christ, the Spirit causes you to become adopted as God's forever child. Nothing can take away your status as His adopted child.

Have you entered into God's family? If so, you have brothers and sisters you did not have before. Your eternal family will be made up of so many Christ followers from around the world that it will take an eternity to get to know them all! If you have been born of the Spirit, you are secure in God's family circle.

Have you been born again into God's family? If so, at that moment of rebirth you received God's Spirit within you. Receiving the Spirit is not a second work that happens later. You have all of the Spirit at salvation. The Spirit will slowly get more and more of you as you partner with Him in your becoming more holy.[3]

A boy was removed from a home where there was chemical addiction, fear, and neglect. The boy was then able to spend time with a man and a woman who wanted to adopt him. The boy felt loved by them and liked them.

The court day came. The judge asked the boy, "Son, do you want this man and this woman to be your forever daddy and mommy?"

The boy said, "Yes, sir. Forever, and ever!"

The judge declared the adoption to be final. The boy jumped into his new daddy's arms and reached out to hug his new mama. No more fear! Adopted, forever and ever!

Have you been adopted by the Father?

God's child has a close relationship with Him as "Papa."

Now we call him, "Abba, Father."

Romans 8:15

Jesus and His parents spoke Aramaic in their community. In their spiritual gatherings, they spoke

---

[3] You may hear people use the word sanctification. It is a term used to refer to the Holy Spirit's work of making the believer holy. He makes us wholly acceptable to God at salvation, and then He partners with us in our on-going practice of living sanctified lives, set apart for God's purpose.

Hebrew. In travels of a day's walk, they likely spoke Greek. Jesus spoke three languages, yet his heart language was Aramaic. The word Abba is Aramaic for "Daddy." When Jesus prayed in the garden of Gethsemane, He called His Heavenly Father "Abba." In that same relational warmth and closeness, those who have been truly saved are those who know the Lord up close and personal, and react to His warmth and care. Our Papa takes us into His family room to hang out with Him. We are His kids. We speak the same heart language our Daddy speaks.

Though there is a place for eloquent language when speaking of the majesty of the Lord, those who are His children don't always have to speak with Him formally. You don't have to pray in King James English. Can you imagine one of our sons calling us on the phone and saying, "Oh dearest parental unit, how fare thee on these trepid days of late?"

If you grew up with loving parents as I did, then at an early age you had constant reminders of the Heavenly Father's love for you. It has likely been easy for you to get to know God's tenderness and hear the language of His heart for you.

If you had an earthly father who was a hard taskmaster, often belittling you or negatively comparing you to others, it may be more difficult for you to come to grips with the nature of the Father God. Even so, once you do, you may appreciate Him more than those who did not have your Dad as an earthly father.

Do you know the Lord in the way a child knows an affectionate, tender Daddy? God's child knows Him like that.

God's child has an inner conviction of belonging to God.

For his Spirit joins with our spirit

to affirm that we are God's children.

Romans 8:16

Do you have a sense of God's endorsement within you, that He is saying you are His child? From within the soul, the Holy Spirit helps the true believer be confirmed as truly saved. The Spirit puts God's personal touch into the depths of God's child. The intensity of such confirming by the Spirit can be a breath-taking experience.

Sometimes the Spirit confirms our spirit in a general way, reassuring us that we have been adopted by God. Other times, the Spirit's affirmation of our standing before God comes through His work in a particular life situation. Are you a believer in a marriage that is painful? The Spirit bathes and heals your hurts, confirming that you belong to God. Are you a child of God who is unpopular at work because you won't lower your moral standards? The Spirit lifts you up and encourages you, and in that supernatural boldness given by the Spirit you find a confirmation that you are God's child.

> The Spirit puts God's personal touch into the depths of God's child.

Only God's child has such experiences of the Spirit within, giving an inner conviction of belonging to God.

God's child is ready to share Christ's future glory.

And since we are his children, we are his heirs.

In fact, together with Christ

we are heirs of God's glory.

Romans 8:17

If you are God's child, He has written you into His will. People have a will as they prepare to die. God has a will even though He is not going to die. He is simply preparing to share all He has with all His children once we arrive in heaven. When God shares, the amount He has left never diminishes. He is the great multiplier of unlimited goodness and glory.

God the Father, Son and Spirit are already there in Eternity sharing glory with each other, and are ready to share their glory with God's children. We will share in the reign of God's Kingdom. He will crown us with dignity and honor. We will receive the eternal rewards of our works done for Him while on earth. We will be blessed to cast all those crowns and rewards at His feet in worship of the only One worthy.

Everything you are currently building on earth will decay to dust. Everything you are buying right now while on this earth will end up at the dump. You will not be pulling a U-Haul behind your hearse. There is no self-storage unit on earth beamed up to heaven for you.

If you possess Christ however, in the eternal Kingdom all that is Christ's will be yours! You will become fully super-naturalized, sharing in His power, lifted above the deterioration you knew on earth. You will be living as the child of the One who owns everything and shares it all with you and all His children.

A long time ago, there was a television show featuring Jed Clampett, Ellie May, and Jethro. Do you recall the name of the show? It was *The Beverly Hillbillies*. What a fun show. Jed had become a millionaire without knowing it. After finding out he was wealthy, he tried his hardest to act rich, but never knew just quite how to act.

If you have died to self and let Christ live in you, then you are eternally rich. Do you know how to act like you are rich?

Are you a spiritual Jed Clampett? If you are really His child, and if God could show you through a crystal ball what your inheritance is and how truly rich you already are in Christ, you would likely be living a lot differently right now.

You would not fret over things that moths will eat or rust will destroy. You would invest more into things that will last for eternity. Right now you are rich in His inseparable love, His constant joy, His unshakeable peace, His forever family, and His dazzling glory.

As Jesus' followers, we are co-heirs with Him. The Father raised Jesus, lifted Him into eternity, and exalted

Him. He will do the same for us. When the Son arrived before the Father, the Father rewarded Him for His obedient suffering on earth. After having been faithful through it all, we as well will come before the Father to be rewarded.

We will have meaningful responsibilities given to us in the eternal Kingdom. We will enjoy seeing again believing loved ones who went before us. There will be ample time for interviewing Paul, Peter, Stephen, and every follower of Christ through the centuries. We will produce new praise songs and sing them in every earthly tongue as well as eternity's language. God's mysteries will finally be revealed. All that is God's will be ours. Best of all, we will glisten as reflectors of the Triune God's brilliant glory.

As Gods' child, you are eager and ready to share Christ's future glory because you are already living for Christ's glory now.

God's child is willing to share Christ's current suffering.

But if we are to share his glory,

we must also share his suffering.

Yet what we suffer now is nothing

compared to the glory he will reveal to us later.

Romans 8:17-18

Though you can't always see it while you are in the middle of suffering, the trials you face for Christ's sake purify you and make you more prepared for glory. As a true believer, you become bold through suffering for Christ. Persecution makes you a supernatural super power with which to be reckoned. Knowing Christ in His suffering and in His resurrection power makes you dangerous. Nowhere on earth is there a Christ follower with more spiritual power than one who is persecuted.

Are you a true follower of Christ? Would persecution result in your faithfulness and boldness? Persecuted believers have a Kingdom perspective not found among so-called believers who *say* they have come to the Lord while holding on to the fleshly "what's in it for me?" approach.

Persecution causes "cultural Christians" to revert to culture and forget about being "Christian." Yet if you are a true Christ follower, you are reminded through suffering that you belong to Him, not yourself. You were made for something better than pleasing self in this life. When following Christ makes your life difficult, do you have an *allergic* reaction or an *allegiant* reaction?

> You were made for something better than pleasing self.

Paul wrote to the believers in Rome about sharing Christ's suffering. As they read the letter you are now examining, they were in the middle of some of the most severe persecution you could imagine. The Roman Emperor Nero had literally gone mad and burned Rome, while blaming the fire on Christ followers. He ordered soldiers to capture Christians, roll them alive in tar, then mount them in his vast gardens where they were lit as torches at night. Nero used the impressive Rome coliseum as a place to gather large crowds to be entertained. The crowds went wild cheering on wild beasts he let loose to chase and devour Christ followers. Christ followers not fed to wild beasts might get hung as roadside decorations on all roads leading to Rome. In the early 60s A.D., most all the roads to Rome became lined with crosses on which hung those dying in just the same way as their Master.

Sharing in Christ's suffering is not just something that happened in the first century. Today, there are more persecuted Christ followers than any previous generation.[4] In Communist East Asia, it is forbidden to share the gospel with anyone under the age of eighteen. It is forbidden for a foreigner to "spread spiritual pollution and superstition." Only churches registered by the government with a government trained pastor enjoy so-called "protection."

Even in those churches, no home meetings are allowed and the second coming of Christ cannot be a sermon topic. If these rules are broken, a believer can expect torture, job loss, and imprisonment. In one city recently, an athletic stadium was filled with spectators watching dozens of Christ followers being shot in the back of their heads one by one. In the Middle East, it is not the government but the new believer's own family members who are ready to perform the execution, often by stoning.

---

[4] https://www.opendoorsusa.org/christian-persecution/stories/11-christians-killed-every-day-for-their-decision-to-follow-jesus/

If you were to ask those believers how you can pray for them what might they say? Would they say, "Pray for our suffering to cease?" That is not their request. They pray that God will give them holy boldness to be invisible to the enemy yet remain faithful unto death if required. They pray that even in dying for Christ, others would be moved to live for Him.

If you are a true Christ follower, you won't shy away from Christ when following Him makes your life more difficult. Willingness to suffer for Christ shows you are born again and have a servant mentality. Even if it causes you to suffer in some way, you will be bold and faithful to the One who suffered for you. You will be dangerous.

Pray for your brothers and sisters in Christ who are persecuted around the world today. Unwillingness to suffer for Christ shows you may still have the entitlement mentality of a person not yet born again.

What can earth do to you if you are guaranteed the rich glory of heaven? *To fear suffering for Christ is like a millionaire fearing the loss of a penny*. Whatever little temporary losses you may endure for Christ on earth is nothing in comparison to all that is yours to gain in Eternity.

Discussion Questions

1. Is professing belief that Christ is the Savior the same as possessing Christ through committing your life to Him?

Do you profess or do you possess Christ?

Who possesses you?

2. Read Romans 8:14. Do you experience the Spirit's personal leading in your daily life?

How?

3. Read Romans 8:15. Do you see God as close and loving, or as distant and dreadful?

Do you see yourself as adopted into God's family, as His child, with brothers and sisters in Christ?

Do you have a close relationship with God as your "Papa"?

4. Read Romans 8:16. Do you have within you an inward conviction of God's Spirit affirming that you are God's child?

5. Read Romans 8:17. If God could show you, maybe through a "crystal ball," your glorious future inheritance, how would you live differently now?

6. For a Christ follower to fear suffering, in light of the glory soon to come, is like a millionaire fearing the loss of a penny.

How willing are you now to share Christ's current sufferings?

7. *Insert your name in the following declaration:*

(_____) is moved by the impulses of the Holy Spirit.

(_____) did not receive the spirit of religious duty, leading me back into the fear of never being good enough.

(_____) is not an orphan. I will not feel orphaned for as He rises up within me, my spirit joins Him in saying the words of tender affection, "Beloved Father."

(_____) has received the Spirit of full acceptance enfolding me into the family of God.

The Spirit makes God's fatherhood real to (_____), as He whispers into my innermost being, "(_____), you are my beloved child!"[5]

---

[5] Based on Romans 8:14-16 TPT

The entire universe is standing on tiptoe,

yearning to see the unveiling of God's glorious

sons and daughters! For against its will the universe itself

has had to endure the empty futility resulting from the

consequences of human sin.

But now, with eager expectation,

all creation longs for freedom from its slavery to decay

and to experience with us the wonderful freedom

coming to God's children. To this day we are aware of the

universal agony and groaning of creation,

as if it were in the contractions of labor for childbirth. And

it's not just creation.

We who have already experienced the first fruits

of the Spirit also inwardly groan as we passionately long to

experience our full status as God's sons and daughters—

including our physical bodies being transformed.

For this is the hope of our salvation.

But hope means that we must trust and wait

for what is still unseen. For why would we need to hope for

something we already have? So because our hope is set on

what is yet to be seen,

we patiently keep on waiting for its fulfillment.

Romans 8:19-25 TPT

Creation Helps God's Child
Become Fully Alive

Do you remember the Johnny Cash story from an earlier chapter? When Johnny went deep into a cave in order to die, what did God use to help Johnny live? Here's a hint. God used something that is a part of nature. Still struggling to remember? He felt something, which gave him a rush of unexpected hope. It was as if God were telling him there was a reason to continue living. In that moment through an act of nature, deep in a dark cave, Johnny experienced the reality of God with Him.

Cash flipped from desiring death to craving life. He had climbed down deep into the earth. How could he possibly find his way out of the maze of dark caves? What did God use to help Johnny? *A gentle breeze* started blowing on his face, giving him hope and guiding him out. Johnny followed the breeze to daylight and to new life in Christ. Creation is a gentle breeze that helps God's child want to become fully alive.

Few people are seeing the big picture of God's future purpose for His created world. Conservationists are feverishly trying to save nature from man's destruction. God is not out to save the earth. He is out to recreate it. The earth as we know it will one day be a goner.

Evolutionists are out to prove the earth came about by a random series of events without any intelligent designer. It's like saying the wind blew through a junk yard and just so happened to create a 747 jet. It takes great faith for anyone to hold on to such a belief. The more the details are examined, the more evidence pointing toward intelligent design.

Others think we should worship "mother earth." Yes, the created earth has a sense of awe about it. Yet worshipping creation is like seeing an intricately designed watch and admiring the watch more than the watch maker.

Many people are not concerned about conserving the earth, proving her origin, or worshipping her. The masses of stressed-out earth dwellers just want escape from the tough realities of this world.

Where is there anything more than human suffering on a suffering planet? Is there any hope for us and for this disintegrating planet? Feel God's gentle breeze on your face and be hopeful.

Actually, there *is* certain hope for this earth. God is about to do something incredible with His creation and His people. Creation seeks to stir within us a yearning for the future Kingdom, where things will finally be as they were intended.

God's created universe is headed toward His eternal purpose. It's time for us to see creation in a fresh, Biblical, future-oriented perspective. Through simultaneously renewing creation and His true followers, the Lord will usher in His Kingdom. In the Kingdom to come, creation will forever help God's children be fully alive. Even now, creation is doing just that.

Creation's original purpose was to help mankind be fully alive.

For all creation is waiting eagerly for that future day

when God will reveal who his children really are.

Against its will, all creation

was subjected to God's curse.

But with eager hope, the creation looks forward

to the day when it will join God's children

in glorious freedom from death and decay.

For we know that all creation

has been groaning as in the pains of childbirth

right up to the present time.

Romans 8:19-22

Suffering easily takes the life out of you. So when Paul writes to the suffering believers in Rome, there is a continual focus on helping people become fully alive.

Suddenly the topic seems to shift from God's children to creation.

I sat in my study and wondered, "What does creation have to do with people becoming fully alive?" I got up from the desk, left that very question written with a big question mark in place on my study notes, and went with twelve pastor friends on a four-day backpacking hike along the Appalachian trail.

Way out there away from the stresses of everyday life and away from my cell phone, I found myself relaxing and enjoying having no schedule or demands beyond survival. Each night around the campfire, we swapped stories that pastors can only tell other pastors! Out there in nature I felt fully alive, especially after a bear walked through our camp one night!

Once back to my desk in civilization and back at the task of this chapter, I looked down at my study notes to see the scribbled question; *What does creation have to do with becoming fully alive?* I had somehow forgotten the awesome rejuvenating effect of being out in God's creation. Time on the Appalachian trail had been God's gentle breeze across my soul.

The word "creation" is repeated four times in these four verses of Romans eight. Many researchers are examining how nature got here. The word "creation" itself means that a Creator is required. The Origin of all species is the One, True Creator God.

Why did He create this earth and this universe? God created a universe so amazing that it would require giving praise to the One who designed it. He created the earth so that man would cultivate it, multiply people on the earth, and have dominion over it. (Gen. 1:26-28)

Are humans simply one of many life forms? Are all life forms equal without a superior life form among the species? Is a cactus or a frog of equal value to a human? This is a common idea shared in many classrooms today; that all life forms, including humans, are equal. Really?

God made man as the crown of all His created creatures. Only *human* life was created in the very image of God Himself (Gen. 1:27) You and I are not slightly altered fish that sprouted legs and arms.

There is no doubt that species do change over time to adapt to their environment. Yet the evolving of life forms does not demand belief that in the beginning there was no intelligent design. In fact, the incredible mathematical intricacies of the universe point strongly toward intelligent design of the universe.

Though we commonly say we *created* something, the definition of the word created is to make something *from nothing*. We can't do that. We make something out of this, that, and the other thing. Creation by definition is "ex nihilo," or "out of nothing." Darwinism, according to Lee Strobel in his book, *The Case for a Creator*, is very farfetched; too farfetched to be credible. Darwinism believes that non-life produced life at random.

After examining scientific evidence from many angles, including cosmology, physics, astronomy, biochemistry, DNA, and consciousness, Strobel concludes all the evidence points clearly toward a living, intelligent designer as Creator. Darwin said that if someone were to find life that can't breakdown, then Darwin's theory would break down. San Francisco Biophysicist Dean Kenyon and many other scientists concur that since Darwin's time many amazing life forms have been found that won't breakdown. At that point, Darwinism breaks down.

Original creation had perfect peace without conflict, order without chaos, harmony without disease, happiness without misery, and management without disrepair. The garden of Eden was a palace for the residence of creation's ruler; mankind. Creation was intelligently designed by God to help mankind be fully alive. The beautiful earth God originally created was the dream home of all dream homes.

Here's a challenge. Within the next week, intentionally spend less screen time and more outdoor time. Try to block out an entire portion of one day to spend time outside, disconnected from demands. See if creation doesn't help you become more fully alive.

Creation can hardly wait for God's real children to be revealed.

But with eager hope,

the creation looks forward to the day when

it will join God's children

in glorious freedom

from death and decay.

Romans 8:20-21

In the original Greek language, *eager hope* describes straining forward with intensity. There is an eager, confident hope, an expectant waiting. Every morning our thirteen ducks somehow know we are about to open the garage door and feed them. They start making the most excited clatter. When the door opens they crowd around, barely leaving us enough room to maneuver between them as we carry their food out to the grass. They scurry in a hurry to follow us, straining their necks, ready for what is to come from their master.

Creation says, "I'm not at rest! I'm leaning forward on the front of my seat to see God's future. I'm so eager to see glorified Christ followers free of sin's decay and death. I was created to be the home for people who reflect God's glory. I can't wait to do what I was intended to do. I'm ready and waiting for God to recreate this earth into recreated man's forever home."

After all we have done to harm her, you would think creation would not want to have anything to do with us humans, yet we see that creation's attitude toward man is the same as her Creator's attitude toward man: unmerited favor. Amazingly, despite all we have done to her, creation herself can hardly wait for God's real children to be revealed. Not only that, creation is willing and ready to give us a second chance at being her ruler.

I can just imagine creation looking us right in the eyes as she says, "Together, you and I, creation and creature, will become dazzling reflections of Christ's glory. So, God's children, I ask you, in light of my future as your future home, how will you treat me now? Wouldn't it be in the best interest of both of us if my waters were not polluted with plastic, my lands not the dumping grounds of deadly toxins, and my skies not filled with carbon monoxide? I am so ready for my Creator to make me right again and recreate me into a proper home for those who have been recreated by Christ and been given recreated bodies."

Creation now is like a coiled spring tightly compressed, eagerly straining forward, ready to be released into her totally restored version. She is excited about her glorious future as the home of God's glorified people. She is ready and waiting to see us revealed as God's children. In light of how eager creation is for eternity, how can we sit around talking about our jobs, our houses and cars, our aches and pains, football, the stock market, and online shopping deals, as if this world is all there is?

> Together creation and creature will become dazzling reflections of Christ's glory.

Have you truly become God's child? Do you groan from the decaying effects that sin has on you? Have you begun now to see creation as groaning under the effects of man's sin? Are you, like creation, eager for the day when God's people and the created world will be glorified together into an eternity of God's marvelous light and glory?

Creation feels the frustration of her purpose being prevented.

Against its will,
all creation was subjected to God's curse.

Romans 8:20a

Creation groans because her God-given rulers fell into sin. That's when she sprouted thorns, thistles and stingers. Prior to sin all creatures great and small were kind and helpful to man. After sin, animals revolted and became under the bondage of cruel instincts. The natural world we now live in is not normal. This world is not what it was made to be.

Creation says, "I'm not what I ought to be. The Creator fashioned me to be a symphony of praise to Him, but for now He's allowed my band to stay on the bus. I've got a great stereo amp but my volume is temporarily muted by sin. Until sin is a thing of the past, I won't stop suffering."

Creation is decaying, staggering like a drunk. She is trembling like a tent in a storm. The handiwork of God is crumbling apart. Earth longs to be restored.

A doll house rests in a moving box in our garage. The elaborate structure once belonged to my wife's grandmother. In its day, it was a sight to behold. Delicate hand-carved wood porches lined the front and back of the house. Each room had hand-crafted doll-size furniture. It was a beautiful display of the skill of a master wood craftsman. But now we are afraid to even take it out of the box. It has become so old and decayed, much of the house has literally fallen into pieces. But just you wait and see. A promise has been made to the one who loves that house and longs for it to be restored. One day soon, my Cheryl will not be disappointed!

God's children are moving on up one day soon to a mighty fine house. The Creator is excited and preparing for the move. We ought to be excited about our future home. Even the home herself is eager for us to move in once renovations occur. In fact, creation is trying to bust out right now into her newly created future-self for our sake, but God is holding her back saying, "Not just yet!"

Soon a magnificently recreated earth will be spread out before God's people, and we ourselves will be dazzling, radiant, immortal, pulsating reflections of God's perfection. Are you God's child through faith in Christ as Lord over who you are? How well does your day by day attitude about life in these trying times reflect that you realize the Father's great future for you? Is there *really* any room for gloom?

Until creation is recreated as a new home for God's people, this created earth remains burdened under the sin we continue to inflict on her. She is subjected to the curse of sin against her own will. This passage speaks of creation having a will, an expressive voice, feelings, desires, and personality. Creation takes personally both her present suffering and her future glory.

Creation groans with birth pangs, preparing for the arrival of ... twins!

But with eager hope, the creation looks forward to the day

when it will join God's children in glorious freedom

from death and decay. For we know that all creation

has been groaning as in the pains of childbirth

right up to the present time.

Romans 8:20-22

One day soon, God will take off the restraints from pregnant creation, and she will burst forth with two new arrivals.

The first arrival? *Earth*, completely recreated with a totally new design.

The second arrival? *God's people*, in glorified form fit for eternity.

This globe will be completely renovated into a new and different model. The earth will be recreated as the home of everything happy, free, vigorous, healthy, and pure. Right now, the earth seems old, squeaky, and tired. On that day when God ushers in eternity, this earth will become beautiful, strong, green, and clean. This world is going to give birth to a new version of herself.[6]

The current pain and pangs are not without meaning. The earth is getting more and more pregnant, expecting. Twins are to arrive soon! First, a new earth will arrive as a home for the second arrival, God's people. Like anyone pregnant, creation is eager for all this to hurry up and happen. A recreated earth will soon be spread out as a new home for all who know Christ!

Are you God's child? Are you living as if this current scene is all there is? A new home is being prepared

---

[6] For a more complete description of the new earth, read Revelation 21.

for you even as you read this! Don't focus so much on something so temporary and fleeting as this world. You and I are just passing through. Focus on your destination, on getting in good spiritual shape for eternity, on partnering with creation to be a more fully alive Christ follower, and on inviting others to come along toward eternity. Those without Christ as Lord of their lives will miss out on eternity with God, and will miss out on seeing the beauty of this earth perfectly recreated.

As you notice the world around you, in what specific ways can you sense that creation is in a state of preparation? When can you hear her groaning?

Since creation is expecting, we also should yearn for the delivery.

Not only that, but we ourselves,

who have the first fruits of the Spirit,

groan inwardly as we wait eagerly

for our adoption as sons,

the redemption of our bodies.

For in this hope we were saved;

but hope that is seen is no hope at all.

Who hopes for what he can already see?

But if we hope for what we do not yet see,

we wait for it patiently.

Romans 8:23-25

Not only is creation having birth pangs, but so are God's children. We are standing on tip-toe waiting for the completion of our adoption by God the Father. There is a day coming when we will see Him face to face. Since through His Spirit He has already saved our souls, we know that really soon He will make new our bodies and fit us for eternity with Him. This is the great certain hope we have had since the day we became His. For now, we wait and anticipate.

Notice how much groaning occurs in these verses. Creation groans. We groan. The Spirit groans. We all anticipate the day when all things become as they should be.

C.S. Lewis reminds us that God will make the feeblest and filthiest Christ followers into gods and goddesses-dazzling, radiant, immortal, pulsating all through with such energy and joy and wisdom and love as we cannot now imagine. We will be bright mirrors, reflecting perfectly back to God His own power and delight and goodness.

Since all creation is on tip-toe to see the children of God be released together with the earth into God's delightful goodness, *how should we then live?* As God's children we should be eager for the day when we will come into our own. Soon, both creation and God's children will be released together into glorious times ahead. Meanwhile, our joyful anticipation should deepen day by day. Along with creation, we feel the birth pangs. These broken bodies of ours yearn for the birth of a non-decaying eternal version of ourselves. The longer we wait the larger we become in pregnancy, and the more joyful should be our expectant state.

Discussion Questions

1. Describe a time when it seemed like God became more real to you as you spent time outdoors enjoying the nature He created.

2. In Romans 8:19-25, the created world is personified, with a will, feelings, a voice, and desires. If nature could speak, what might we hear her say?

3. Read Romans 8:19-21. Amazingly, despite all we have done to harm her, creation herself can hardly wait for God's real children to be revealed. She is eager to be fully restored to her original state and become the eternal home of God's glorified people. Through this chapter, in what ways are you seeing creation in a fresh, Biblical perspective?

4. Read Genesis 1:26-28. According to Romans 8:20, right now creation is frustrated. In what ways does nature suffer because of man's sin?

5. Read Romans 8:22. Are you God's child through faith in Christ as Lord over who you are? How well does your day by day attitude about life in these trying times reflect that you realize the Father's great future for you? Is there any room for gloom?

6. Read Romans 8:23-25. Since all creation is on tip-toe to see the children of God be released together with the earth into God's delightful goodness, how should we then live?

7. In what ways does creation, even now, help God's child become fully alive?

And in a similar way,

the Holy Spirit takes hold of us

in our human frailty

to empower us in our weakness.

For example, at times we don't even know how to pray,

or know the best things to ask for.

But the Holy Spirit rises up within us

to super-intercede on our behalf,

pleading to God with emotional sighs

too deep for words.

God, the searcher of the heart,

knows fully our longings,

yet he also understands the desires of the Spirit,

because the Holy Spirit passionately pleads before God

for us, his holy ones,

in perfect harmony with God's plan and our destiny.

Romans 8:26-27 TPT

Seven Keys to Praying

In the ~~Flesh~~ Spirit

It's confession time. I, Matthew, pastor for more than forty years, just don't seem to have the ability to pray effectively. In the middle of prayer, I have often become unsure of what to pray next. Sometimes my mind drifts while praying. I have also abused prayer as a means of getting something across to *people* instead of conversing with *God*. I don't know how to pray as I should. Now, I've admitted it. And I feel better for at least having stated right up front my prayer inadequacies.

Am I the only one feeling like my prayers sometimes bounce off the ceiling? Once when I asked a deacon to pray during a prayer meeting, he said, "Oh, I let my wife do that sort of thing." I didn't have the heart to get tough on the guy, but instead said, "Understood. My wife is also much better at talking with God than I am."

113

During Vacation Bible School, I asked a children's leader to pray at our assembly, and she replied, "I don't know any prayers."

"Yes," I replied, "sometimes I feel that way as well. It reminds me of when I was dating a young lady for the first time. I didn't know what to talk about so I wrote out a script before calling her."

It seems that most followers of Christ in a moment of honest reflection would agree that prayer is sometimes challenging. Were it left up to the abilities of our own flesh, it would be very difficult to have meaningful dialogue with Someone who is not sitting in front of us in the flesh.

Jesus rebukes those who pray to impress others, as if superior spirituality is measured by eloquent words.[7] Some prayers are scripted for human ears, with verbiage designed to inflate the status of the one making fleshly utterances.

We may also be praying in the flesh if we see prayer as asking God for what we want. "Lord, not thy will but mine be done." A fleshly demand made and claimed in prayer puts self as sovereign and turns God into an on-demand vending machine. Got something you want? Just take it to God, the Sanctified Santa.

After counseling a dating couple, I asked them to pray together. The young man began. "Lord, please help me know how far I can go with my girl and still not be sinning." After the "amen," he asked me if he prayed for the wrong thing.

---

[7] Luke 20:46-47. See also Matthew 23:13-39.

Though his prayer smelled like flesh, I said, "Honest prayer is never the wrong thing to do. You are seeking God's thoughts instead of seeking advice from your peers, who might say to go all the way with her now instead of waiting for marriage."

Whenever anyone fumbles at prayer, my heart goes out to them with full sympathy. I simply know how they feel. I have repeatedly tested positive for PDSD - Prayer Deficient Saint Disease.

What is the invisible secret of effective prayer? The secret is that our weakness is *exactly* what God uses to show us His strength! God does not mind clumsy praying. In fact, He loves the simplest of prayers, whether voiced by young children or by feeble senior adults.

The entrance into the invisible place of communion with God is a very low door, entered only by a heart bowing low. The secret of real prayer is that weakness in prayer gives the Spirit the opportunity to engage in helping us talk with the Father.

Unfortunately, some Christ followers seldom if ever enter in to the secret of communing with God. Without entrance into that invisible place, we pray "in the flesh."

When we pray with sensitivity to what the Spirit within is saying to us, we are praying "in the Spirit."[8] *The secret to an invisible soul to soul connection with our Creator is engaging the help of His Spirit within us.* Praying in the Spirit begins with waiting on Christ in the heart to prompt the utterances to be made with the lips.

---

[8] See Ephesians 6:18-20 and Jude 1:17-23.

The Holy Spirit wants to be your personal prayer coach. If you suffer from PDSD, by encouraged about the powerful possibility hidden within your feeble prayer ability.

Praying in the Spirit wakes you up. We have heard children pray at night, "If I should die before I wake..." With the Spirit praying through you, you will find yourself waking up before you die!

> Prayer in the Spirit begins with waiting on Christ in the heart to prompt the utterances made with the lips.

By praying in the Spirit, you will find yourself praying what you would not have otherwise prayed. You will discover power, freedom of speech, and intimacy with God. Instead of trying to think of the right thing to say, the Holy Spirit will help you hear what God has to say. He will also bring to your mind what needs to be brought to the Father. The Spirit intercedes for you before the Father. The Spirit will be praying *with* you, *for* you and *through* you.

Let's explore seven questions which reveal seven keys to praying in the flesh Spirit. Here's the first one.

Do you realize your prayer life needs the Spirit's help?

...The Holy Spirit

helps us...

Romans 8:26

Is prayer for you merely a meal time, church time, bedtime ritual? Sure you pray, but do you only get down on your knees in humble desperation as the final step when all else fails and "there's nothing to do now but pray"?

You need help. Everyone around you clearly sees you need help. ⍰ Admit it. But where can you get the help you need? Your help comes from the Lord. Say out loud, "Lord, I need help." You get the Lord's help through prayer. Say, "Holy Spirit, help me pray."

Maybe one area where you need help is understanding yourself. If you keep getting into disposable relationships, ask the Spirit to help you understand why. Ask the Spirit why you have unmet needs. Ask Him why you often feel empty, weary, fearful, and insecure.

You will be amazed how prayer in the Spirit will give you the Father's insight into your life. Whatever particular personal issues you may be facing today, Spirit directed prayer will...

... help you see your heart struggles from the Father's perspective

.... open up your limited thinking to see new God-sized possibilities

... cause you to see how God is at work through your circumstances

... bring emotional and relational healing otherwise impossible

Does God seem far away? Such a feeling is false. *He is very near.* Yet the feeling of God being distant may linger within because you haven't been effectively communicating with Him. The Spirit is ready and waiting to be your Helper with that problem. We feel close to those

117

with whom we talk regularly. Let the Spirit help you start talking with the Father, unscripted.

Feeling like no one really understands what you are going through? If you are in relationship with Christ, then His Spirit within you *does* understand, and He is on stand-by. He is waiting for you to ask for His help in sorting it out. Ask for His help already! He is the only one who truly gets it. He understands you better than you do!

> True prayer comes from a heart humbled enough to seek help in having real conversation with the Father.

The first key to praying in the Spirit instead of the flesh is to *realize your prayer life needs the Spirit's help*. True prayer comes from a heart humbled enough to seek the indwelling Spirit's help in having real conversation with the Father. Do you realize your prayer life needs the Spirit's help?

Have you arrived yet at shattered self-sufficiency?

And the Holy Spirit

helps us in our *weaknesses...*

Romans 8:26

Do you feel that you are on top of the details of your life?

Are you deceived into feeling capable of handling life in your own strength and wisdom?

I've got this thing; I'm well aware of what needs to happen. I'm making it happen.

Do you ask God to make you strong? Instead, pray *Lord, give me the strength to be weak.*

If you think you are strong then you won't receive God's blessings. His blessings don't arrive until life humbles you. Even then, to be helped you must see that you *need* help. You must admit weakness.

It's best for you to realize early on that you are weak. Open up yourself quickly to willingly and eagerly receive God's help.

Weak or strong? Which describes you?

Most all of us live under the illusion that we are captains of our own ships. It often takes a crisis to change our minds. COVID was just such a crisis. God used COVID to shatter human self-sufficiency. Through COVID, many of us came to realize our weakness. We are people of frailty. Our fingers do not have a sovereign snap causing our lives to go back to pre-COVID days.

If a crisis has left you *confused, overwhelmed, and helpless,* you are right where God wants you to be, minus the confusion.

If all you have now is *empty hands*, lift them up to God.

If you only have a *heart full of anguish*, pour it out before Him.

If you have a *deep, unspeakable need*, cry out to God.

Life is not about always being certain of what to do and how to do it. It's about Who you ask to guide you through this world of uncertainty and deadly crises. The moment death's shadow shatters your self-sufficiency – *that's* the moment the Spirit helps you to become fully alive. Arrive as early as you can at the point of shattered self-sufficiency. There at that hidden place the Spirit is waiting for you to come ask for His help.

The Christ-life is not getting saved then simply doing the best you can with what you have. Following Christ means realizing the futility of self-effort and replacing it with admitted weakness in reliance on the Spirit's power.

The exchanged life places Spirit-reliance in the place of self-reliance. That exchange of control is not at all easy. It feels like a risky exchange. Self-reliance is a comfortable place to abide. We like the illusion that we are in control of outcomes based on our own effort.

To make the exchange, we must relinquish control and become unsure of outcomes. Life, in all its complexity, goes into the hands of Someone we honestly aren't sure we can trust to handle it better than we could.

Yet after making the exchange it usually isn't long before our worries are put to rest. Life reliant on the Spirit puts self in much more capable hands. Life in the Spirit gets us beyond the inconsistencies of self. A far greater power fills us with the ability to overcome the temptations of the flesh.[9]

---

[9] The weakness mentioned in Romans 8:26 refers first to our inability to overcome fleshly desires mentioned in Romans 7, then also to our inability to pray without the Spirit's help.

Spirit-led prayer empowers us to live a life that blesses us and others. Ours is a holy life. We enjoy the benefits of a close connection to our Creator. We live set apart for His pleasure. All is well with the soul.

When we walk in the Spirit instead of the flesh, life becomes a Spirit-directed dialogue with the Father that goes all day and night without an "amen" adjourning us back to self-directed living. We find ourselves regularly stirred to seek the Father rather than the things of this world or the opinions of others. The Spirit develops new thought patterns in our minds as we begin to live and move by the promises of God. Boldness we never knew before makes us dangerous to the enemy, even though we may be few. Our personalities are becoming super-naturalized, developing character in our lives only the Spirit can produce.[10]

Self is too weak to withstand evil, too weak to obey God. As a self-directed individual, you yourself are too weak to live a moral life. Self is too weak to consistently take a stand for what is right. Isn't it time to come to the end of self?

名词

The Chinese word 名词 "crisis" (위기) is made up of two characters: danger and opportunity. A crisis is a dangerous opportunity. The opportunity? A rare chance for death-producing self-direction to be replaced with becoming fully alive through the Spirit. The dangers? Risking change or refusing the opportunity.

The second key to praying in the Spirit instead of the flesh is to *come to a place of crisis*

---

[10] See Galatians 5:22-23

where self-sufficiency is shattered. True prayer begins when we admit our weakness and ask for the Spirit's power to help us in connecting with the Father. Have you arrived at that place of shattered self-sufficiency?

Do you know that you don't know how to pray as you should?

And the Holy Spirit helps us in our weakness.

For example, *we don't know* what

God wants us to pray for.

Romans 8:26

One time Jesus asked someone with an obvious need, "What do you want me to do for you?" Couldn't Jesus see what needed done? Certainly. Yet Jesus wanted the person to think about his true need, and humbly ask the Lord for help.

The Lord knows what we need, even though it may not be obvious to *us* what we need. God wants us to see our *real* needs. What we see as the main issue may only be a surface issue revealing something deeper. We may not even have realized the issue is down there. Only the Spirit's help brings it up.

I recently asked the people gathered in a worship center, "What are you asking God to do?" They looked around at the few number of people attending worship and said, "That's obvious. These empty seats need to be full."

When God told Gideon to conquer the enemy, Gideon started thinking he needed lots of people. God then reduced Gideon's army from 22,000 to 300, causing

Gideon to see the battle is not won by might nor by power but by God's Spirit. The 22,000 were Gideon's but the 300 were God's.[11]

Could it be that the church is praying for the wrong things? Are we praying out of the flesh for the big reputation of the church to be restored? Do we care more about getting people in a church building than being the body of Christ, the hands and feet of Jesus out among people in need?

How does it strike God's ears when we pray for him to rest more bottoms in more church pews? Were we to ask the Spirit how to pray, might we find ourselves praying for God to reduce us to the faithful few who will get off our bottoms and go out in victory to win people into His kingdom?

We pray amiss when we ask God to strengthen us. We should instead agree with God on our weakness and His great strength. Without recognizing our weakness, we tackle life head-on, like a battering ram.

> We pray amiss when we ask God to strengthen us.

We are prone to tackle life with full force by using our own intellect, connections, will power, and a bit of prayer sprinkled on top. We see the enemy. He's behind a gate. We think we must knock that gate down. We gather all we've got and yell, "Charge!" The dust flies as we stampede. But when the dust settles, the gate still stands.

Praying in the Spirit changes all that. He has us camp outside the wall of the enemy, wait, and keep looking to Him. One day, the draw bridge simply goes up, the enemy walks out defeated and says, "We surrender!"

---

[11] See Judges 6:33-7:15.

Praying in the Spirit is like that. It lets God do the fighting for us. The Spirit helps us know which are true battles and which are not. The Spirit leads the fight and tells us how to get involved and how *not* to get involved. It's time to let God fight for us through Spirit-led prayer.

The third key to praying in the Spirit instead of the flesh is to *know that you don't know how to pray*. True prayer never assumes you see the situation the same way God does.

If we think we know how to pray, we may be praying for methods God does not bless, for outcomes God does not desire, or for strength He chooses not to display until our weakness is obvious. Do you know that you don't know how to pray?

Do you ask the Spirit to influence your dialogue with the Father?

We don't know what

God wants us to *pray* for.

Romans 8:26

In the New Testament original language, the word *pray* used here is Προσεύχομαι, pronounced "proseuchomai", which literally means to interact with the Lord, to dialogue with the Divine, to have conversation with God. *Pros* means toward, and *euchomai* is the root of the word Eucharist or communion. Prayer is to enter into communion with God. Are you having two-way conversations with the Father?

124

Without the Spirit's involvement, prayer is one way. We fill up the conversation with our own voice and end the conversation without giving God a chance to say anything.

Someone calls you and blabs the whole time, never asks about you, and then says, "Gotta go! By!" How do you feel? Now you know how God feels much of the time!

When you ask for the Spirit of God within you to help you truly commune with God, the Spirit quietens you. He stills you. He directs you to first be still and know that He is God. He then prompts you to ask, "Spirit, what is it that You want to say to me? I'm settled, open-hearted, humble, and listening."

When you enter in to the secret quiet place of Spirit-directed conversation with God, you will find yourself eager to set aside ample time for uninterrupted stillness in God's presence. You will value as the most important part of your day *the sacred silence of simply enjoying being before God* with no agenda other than asking Him to make Himself known to you. Ask Him to help you experience His holiness, His awesomeness, His power, His love, His glory, His shalom,[12] and His contagiousness.

> Carve out a regular time and secret place of quietness to simply enjoy being with God.

Instead of coming to God with an agenda, ask "Spirit, what pleases You?"[13] Jesus, what is Your agenda for me? Father, as a kid of the King who am I to be? Do

---

[12] Shalom means peace, wholeness, well-being, harmony with self, others, and God.

[13] The New Testament church often asked that very question before taking any action. See Acts 15:28.

whatever You need to do within me to make me more fully set apart for You Lord."

In prayer, wait on God. Ask Him to reveal to you what matters concern Him. Don't box in your prayers within man-made parameters. God is too big for any box you try to put Him in. Instead, let the all-powerful, all-knowing, all-present God broaden your borders as you get to know His limitless, supernatural life. He longs to give you life here and now as you spend time with Him.

The fourth key to praying in the Spirit instead of the flesh is to *listen long to the Spirit so that He redirects your prayers* in God's direction not your own. True prayer is letting God speak his agenda first instead of starting with your agenda.

Carve out a regular time and secret place of quietness to simply enjoy being with God and letting Him speak to you. Listen all day for His voice. Do you ask the Spirit to influence you as to what to pray?

Do you let the Spirit make prayers out of your agonizing groans?

The Holy Spirit prays for us

with *groanings*

that cannot be expressed in words.

Romans 8:26

Though you may have trouble conversing with the Father God in heaven, the Spirit within prays for you. God the Spirit within you communicates for you with God the Father. Just how does the Spirit do so?

Human languages are all limited in providing us with a full range of expression of our deepest feelings. Sometimes it takes grunts and groans to express agony, full throttle snorts to express frustrations, and explosive yelps to release great joy. Sometimes we can't even make sounds which adequately express our mixed emotions.

When we are in tune with Him, the Spirit takes all that we feel and communicates it to the Father in heaven's perfect, fully expressive language beyond words. Our spirit and the Holy Spirit unite as one, to make a profound emotional expression heard and fully understood by the Father.

Has your child wandered away from the path, leaving you so brokenhearted you can't describe it? Ask the Spirit to give you outward emotional expression of your inner grief which He will take before the Father for you.

After being told you are barren, are you now holding your healthy, first-born child? You are experiencing one of life's finest moments. Be fully alive by letting out that ecstatic expression of joy before the Father through the Spirit.

Are you in a hospital bed at home on hospice care? Is someone reading these words to you because you no longer have sight nor presence of mind to read? Do you lack the strength to utter a sentence to your caregiver or voice even the simplest prayer to God? Do you have feelings within you want to convey to God? The Spirit prays for you with groanings too deep for words.

> Becoming fully alive requires full expression before God of the range of emotions within you.

Superficial got-it-all-together prayers may sound eloquent to human ears. Yet

127

those who cry out in brokenness with moans get through to God. Groaning is *not* an immature prayer phase you grow out of. Becoming fully alive requires full expression before God of the range of emotions within you. That takes much vulnerability and maturity.

Without letting the Spirit bring all your emotions before the Father, you are nothing but emotionally numb, like Dr. Spock of Star Trek. You have nothing but superficial religiosity when you pray. Is that really what you want? God wants to be in tune with your heart because He wants you to be blessed by His help and presence.

You may have pent-up emotions that are inexpressible in words. You may have deep agonizing longings which never quite come out. Let the Spirit convey your heart to the Father, and let Him convey the Father's heart to you.

The fifth key to praying in the Spirit instead of the flesh is to *let the Spirit make prayers out of your agonizing groans.* True prayer isn't limited to human language. Give yourself freedom to bring all your emotions to the Lord. The Spirit will help convey your innermost self to your Father.

Words are certainly not required while listening to God. Nor are they necessary to express your emotions to God. Sometimes words are over-rated.

Don't settle for prayers that may sound as people expect prayers to sound, without ringing true to what you really feel. Don't worry about what sounds you make. Let it all out before Him. He can handle it. Do you let the Spirit make prayers out of your agonizing groans?

Do you give the Father freedom to search your heart through His Spirit in you?

God, the searcher of the heart,

knows fully our longings,

yet he also understands the desires of the Spirit,

because the Holy Spirit passionately

pleads before God for us, his holy ones...

Romans 8:27a TPT

The Holy Spirit is the Father's powerful search engine roaming every file of your heart you make available to Him. Withholding some files from His search leaves you praying in the flesh. Praying in the Spirit requires giving the Spirit permission to search every hidden place of your heart.

The Google search engine uses an estimated 2,400,000 servers to crawl around in 20 billion websites every single day and night. It performs over 100 billion searches per month.

Yet Google doesn't even begin to compare to the Spirit's search capabilities. Things can hide from Google. Nothing hides from the Spirit. You can *try* to hide from God's Spirit. You can *pretend* you have hidden a part of you. It's like the child who puts a towel over his head and thinks because he can't see others, they can't see him.

There's nothing about you that God's Spirit doesn't already know. There will never be a time when you surprise God with a new revelation about yourself. Since He already knows all about you, you might as well stop trying to hide under a towel.

Unveil your soul. Give the Spirit freedom to search your heart. Eagerly ask Him to reveal your true self. Let Him show you what parts of your heart beat as one with the Father and what parts of your heart are not in tune with God's heart.

Allow Him, and the Spirit will give you a heart tune-up you won't regret. You might not enjoy it while He's doing His exploration inside you. Maybe you won't instantly agree with what He finds. You may not be ready to change in the blink of an eye, but work with Him anyway. Trust Him. Go with His flow, not yours. You will be glad you did. It's the path toward becoming fully alive, toward becoming the you He created you to be.

The sixth key to praying in the Spirit instead of the flesh is to *give the Father freedom to search your heart through His Spirit within you.* True prayer isn't cleaning up a part of your heart and presenting only that side of self to God. Allow God to see the good, the bad, and the ugly within. Let His Spirit work with you to partner toward change for the better.

Don't settle for being stuck with last decade's model of you. You are a new creation, becoming more and more like Christ. That doesn't happen through self-determination. True change requires the power of praying in the Spirit. Do you give the Father freedom to search your heart through His Spirit within you?

Do you ask the Spirit to exchange your desires for God's will?

God, the searcher of the heart, knows fully our longings,

yet he also understands the desires of the Spirit,

because the Holy Spirit passionately pleads before God

for us, his holy ones, in perfect harmony with

God's plan and our destiny.

Romans 8:27 TPT

We often pray in such a way that we are essentially asking God to change His mind. Praying in the Spirit is not like that. Praying in the Spirit changes *our* minds. The Spirit brings us to a point of brokenness before God, where we long for nothing more than His will and His glory regardless of our circumstances. Praying in the Spirit re-directs our wills to conform to the Father's will.

Though you may ask God to change your circumstances, when you pray in the Spirit, what gets changed is *you*. If you allow Him, the Spirit will replace your heavy baggage of self-centered desires with passion for God and for His Kingdom to come. You will find your load lightening as you travel light through this temporary world. You will journey with God in discovering and following His will, whatever it takes and wherever He takes you.

A cancer patient was bitter. She prayed to be cured but became worse. So she finally prayed for God's will to be done through her circumstances. God showed her all the ways she had been blessed by Him throughout life. He made clear the blessing she could be to others in her current circumstance *if she would trust Him* even in cancer.

She wasn't cured, but she was healed of bitterness. A cure is temporary. A healed heart is forever.

The seventh key to praying in the Spirit instead of the flesh is to *ask the Spirit to exchange your desires for God's will.* True prayer isn't getting all you want from God. It is God getting all of you through prayerful surrender to the direction of God's guiding Spirit within you.

When you can't seem to get through to God in prayer, try praying for God to work through the Spirit to conform you to the image of Christ. That's a dangerous prayer. Willingness to change is required. You will become like moldable clay in the Potter's hands. Are you asking the Spirit to exchange your desires for the Father's will?

When you dare to consistently pray in and through the Spirit, you will daily move to God's groove. You will fulfill the plan He made for your specific life, instead of following a course you mapped out for yourself. You will journey with joy toward His unique destiny for you as you become fully alive.

> Are you asking the Spirit to exchange your desires for the Father's will?

Discussion Questions

1. Read Romans 8:26-27, Ephesians 6:18-20 and Jude 1:17-23. From each passage, list some reasons why praying in the Spirit is important.

2. How would you define praying in the flesh? What is praying in the Spirit?

3. Read Romans 8:26-27 in several translations such as the NLT, TPT or the Message Paraphrase. What attitudes are needed for real conversation with the Father?

4. Reflect on times that prayer has not been effective for you. Why was it not? How might the outcome have been different had you prayed differently?

5. Are you carving out regular time to go to a secret place of quietness to simply enjoy being with God?

6. What do you need to do to give God more opportunity to speak to you?

7. Read Acts 15:28. In what specific ways might we the church function differently if at every turn we asked, "What seems good to the Spirit?"

So we are convinced

that every detail of our lives

is continually woven together for good,

for we are his lovers

who have been called

to fulfill his designed purpose.

For he knew all about us

before we were born

and he destined us

from the beginning

to share the likeness of his Son.

This means the Son is the oldest among

a vast family of brothers and sisters

who will become just like him.

Romans 8:28-29 TPT

What Makes Life Good?

There is an African folktale about a king and his friend. The two did everything together. The friend always said, "This is good." One day they went hunting. The friend loaded the king's gun. The king fired the gun, but it backfired and blew off the king's thumb.

The friend said, "This is good."

But the king said, "This is *not* good."

The king sent his friend to prison. A year later, the king went hunting without the friend. On the trip, the king was captured by cannibals and taken to their village. They tied him to a stake.

The king said, "This is not good."

Just before lighting the fire to barbeque the king, one cannibal saw that the king was missing a thumb. As civilized cannibals, they had a rule that they could never eat people who had missing body parts. They untied the king and let him go free.

The king thought of his friend and went to him.

"You were right. It *is* good my thumb was blown off! I should not have thrown you in jail. This is *not* good!"

Yet the friend said, "No. This *is* good. If I had not been in jail, I would have been on that trip with you. And my thumb is not missing!"

We have difficulty defining what is good and what is not. How would you define "the good life?" Is it being forever young and healthy? Is life good when you are wealthy and good looking? If you have a good steady job and a happy family, is *that* the good life? Can the good life only be experienced by a utopian situation? Is there no good life during bad circumstances?

How does good come into a person's life? Ask that question to a small group of random people and the answers might be something like this:

"Well, you work hard. Make a good plan. Work smart and follow your plan."

"That sounds great, but good things go to people who *happen* to be at the right place at the right time and get the lucky breaks."

"What will be will be. Fate decides."

"It's Karma. What you do comes back to you. What goes around comes around."

Is there no other way to look at it? There certainly is! The hand of God is at the helm of what we call circumstances. His hand is attached to His heart, which is set on blessing His people. If we let Him, He will guide us on a path that blesses us even in the middle of tough times.

The good life is becoming fully alive by allowing the Creator to become your life's Composer and Conductor. He will take the noise of your life and create a beautiful symphony! As you follow the Conductor's lead, there are some ways in which you must partner with Him in turning your life into good music. In one fabulous verse of His word to us, we find six ways to experience the good life.

Love God.

"All things work together for the good

of those who *love* God"

Romans 8:28 HCSB

How does life become good? It doesn't… until you love God. The great promise of all things working out for the good cannot be claimed by everyone. There are conditions to the promise. The promise cannot be claimed by those who simply believe the Bible to be true. Nor can it be claimed by those who merely believe that God exists. Even those who simply go to church and strive to live right are not able to claim this promise.

Only those who love God have confidence in who God is. Only those who are no longer living for self now want to please God.

Loving God results in a life aligned with God's plan for you, which results in things turning out for your good, regardless of which way the circumstances may turn. Those who love God willingly suffer the loss of all things to gain Christ, and are not overly concerned with whatever is lost on the way to glory. Those who have given the Lord their highest allegiance trust fully that God's goodness is aimed straight at them in a personalized, tailor-made plan for good despite how things look.

Bethany Hamilton was a typical California teenager who went out to surf, until the particular day of surfing that changed her life. A shark ripped off her arm. Bethany's simple faith in Christ was tested. After some brief struggles with her new identity as perceived by others, she accepted herself as God sees her; complete in Christ.

Bethany's confidence in God's goodness began to soar as she became a much humbler, sweeter, more caring person than before. Now as an adult, Bethany wouldn't trade the loss of an arm for anything. In fact, she thanks God for it.

Tennessee pastor Ray Ortlund Jr. says that love for God is most convincing when offered to Him in the furnace of affliction. Love does not resent affliction. If we love God, we won't stay bitter toward Him even when He allows us to suffer.

Love does not rage against God. Love bows in worship and accepts the will of God with the expectation of good. Does that describe you? Who is the love of your life? Do you understand how much God wants you to love Him?

Say "yes" to God's redirecting call.

"All things work together for the good for…

those who are *called* according to *His purpose*"

Romans 8:28 HCSB

Loving God is the *human side* of the equation. God's redirecting call is the *Divine side*. Make no mistake, God is calling out to everyone to be saved through the cross. God's great big heart of love cries out to all people to come back to our Creator. He is not desiring anyone to leave this earth headed toward an eternity of separation from all things good.

Though He calls out and reaches out to all, only those who say "yes" to His call experience a life that God redirects from darkness to light, from condemnation to freedom, and from gloom to glory. Only those who say "yes" to His call become His called out ones, His chosen ones.

Before hearing God's calling, those who later believed in God were just like anyone else; indifferent toward God. But then God made Himself so real, so nearly unavoidably strong and near, we surrendered our lives to Him, and we started at once to become fully alive to God. His love in us causes us to become fearless for God. His perfect love casts out the dark evil fear which the enemy had us trapped within.

Now we eagerly love Him above all because He first loved us and gave His very best gift to us. We heard His call not as a mere invitation but as a wooing of our hearts to His heart of love for us. Now we look back and are amazed at who God is making us to be compared to before!

Saying "yes" to His call requires willingness for all of life to be set towards a new trajectory, a new direction which turns out to be even better than the old path.

Saying "yes" means saying "no" to lesser things. We set the old aside to become new through asking the Lord to turn us from self and sin. We let Jesus take the captain's chair of our life boat, and we never really miss those old things. Life with the Captain has become much more interesting and meaningful compared to the mere existence we knew before.

Jim was a driven insurance salesman who lived a moral life and was religious. He went to church because it was expected and because it brought business connections. Yet. he had no personal relationship with Christ. His one great love was working hard to sell that next insurance policy. His definition of the good life involved self, money and luxurious pleasure.

Jim's wife was right there by his side until a new friend told her about real life in Christ. She decided to give herself to Jesus. She still gave herself to her husband. In fact, she became such a better version of her former self that Jim, after some hesitation, decided to surrender to the Lordship of Christ as well.

Now as a couple they use their possessions to bless others. Jim is still writing a lot of contracts, but he doesn't live for that purpose. As a couple, they are giving to Kingdom causes more than they ever imagined possible.

Have you experienced the disruption of God calling you? Have you ever been redirected toward the personalized call of God wooing your heart?

Be confident in God's providence.

"We *know* that all things work together for the good…"

Romans 8:28 HCSB

The word *know* in New Testament Greek describes perceiving the meaning of something in your mind. To know all things work together for the good is to live by a settled conviction that the Lord *is* in the details of a person's life. Such conviction makes a person fearless and contagious while the Jesus within becomes nearly unavoidable by those without.

> The good life is built on a love relationship with the Lord.

Those who experience the good life are walking in the dust of Rabbi Jesus, listening to Him, being heard by Him, and following Him wherever He leads. Life as one long conversation led by Jesus is the good life. Being with Jesus and following Jesus results in a conviction so bold, so demanding, so unapologetic that we live sold out for Him, fully invested.

Either God works out everything for the good, or nothing makes sense in life. You either ….

a. have come under the conviction of God's goodness and *surrendered* to Him, resulting in becoming fully alive

or

142

b. you are *trying* to live the good life on your own, yet with no ability to be truly satisfied by the outcome.

Which describes you?

Try, try, try as hard as you want to bring about the good life for yourself. You are just grasping soap bubbles. Stop trying and instead surrender control to Christ. His love will flood into your soul. The good life is built on a love relationship with the Lord, and results in the confidence a child has in his or her Father's arms.

Contrast the "we don't know" of Romans 8:26 with the "we know" of Romans 8:28. We don't know what God wants but we do know *Him*, and we know His heart is bent on causing everything to work out for good for those who love Him. Because of our confidence in knowing Him, we are *not* uptight that we don't know exactly how He wants things to turn out. We should not be assertive about what we *don't* know. But we should never hold back in fear from affirming what we *do* know.

More than a decade ago, my wife Cheryl was diagnosed with brain tumors. We had already served in ministry for more than twenty-five years at that point. Many people seemed afraid that her medical condition might hamper our ministry.

"Pastor, do you think maybe Cheryl's medical condition is affecting your ministry?"

I replied, "There's no maybe about it! Because of her condition, we are more sensitive to people with health concerns. Now we are more caring for people in need. I am a more compassionate husband, father, son, and pastor than before. Now more than ever, Cheryl and I are even more closely tied together as a team."

There's no life like the good life of confidence in God working it all out for the good.

Look for God in all of life's events.

"We know that *all* things..."

Romans 8:28 HCSB

God does not tell us to *merely try to imagine* that all things are good. Much if not most of what surrounds us in this human world is *not* good. So many people are alone. It is not good for man to be alone. It is not good that there is drug addiction, pornography, hatred and violence, poverty, disease, and chemicals polluting the air, land, and water. No, don't live in a dream world that "it's all good" when it's not all good.

Then how in the world can the claim be made that God works it *all* out for the good? Read Romans 8:28. God does not say *some* things or even *most* things work out for good. He doesn't promise that *nice* things work out for good. As difficult as it is to stretch our minds, He is saying that all things...

- evil things
- terrible tragedies
- sudden losses of loved ones
- contagious pandemics
- world-wide unrest

- destructive wildfires
- dark sins
- the worse disappointments
- your hidden hurts

are all sifted through His permissive will, and are all being redirected by the Lord toward His good purpose of making us more like Christ.

God is taking your greatest sorrows, your deepest pain, and your worst failure, and bending them around to serve His good intention toward you. Nothing, absolutely nothing, touches you without His wise permission.

Do you love Him? Have you said "yes" in following the redirecting call of Jesus? If you have, then *every single life event is God at work helping you develop more of the mind of Christ. The result is that life blesses you* from the inside out *regardless of what circumstances try to do to you* from the outside in. Greater is He who is in you than he who is in the world.

You may not physically see the good yet. Here in Tennessee we sometimes hear people say, "You can't never always tell sometimes yet." Not one single life event falls outside God's providence. There is not one single experience that God is not in. Not one event He isn't, right now, turning toward the good. Wait for it. Look for it. Pray for eyes to see it. Expect it. Go on with life confident in it. Be certain that God uses the worst of life for His purpose.

"Has God abandoned me?"

No. Never.

"Have I stepped outside His graceful care?"

Impossible.

"How could my sins be used for good?"

He uses our sins to sting us toward repentance, which is good.

"How could my pain be good?"

If you allow pain to draw you into deeper fellowship with Christ and His suffering for you on the cross, your life story will become a strong tug on the heart of even the most stubbornly self-reliant person. God turns pain into gain.

Are you looking for God in *all* life events?

Watch God orchestrate the noise of life into a symphony.

"All things work *together* for the good..."

Romans 8:28 HCSB

The word "together" in this verse is the root word for the concept we call "synergy." Synergy means combined energies. In synergy there is actually more power together than the sum of the power of each individual part. For instance, one two-by-four might only support two hundred pounds. So, how many pounds would three two-by-fours support? Six hundred pounds. But if the three were to be nailed together as one, how much weight could they hold up? They can hold double what they could individually; one thousand two hundred pounds!

With God in your life, there is no good luck or bad luck, no such thing as a random event. God takes individual parts of our lives which seem unplanned and pulls them together toward His good plan. He mixes them up as one, and causes the combined result to be our good.

Each morning I drink a concoction for my health. When I make the drink, the individual ingredients are almost not edible. I certainly wouldn't eat them individually; things like a frozen banana, some frozen cherries, a tub full of raw baby spinach leaves, fermented mushrooms and, well, you get the idea. When I put them all in the blender, very soon out comes a drink so delicious even our dog Smoky howls begging to drink some of it. Mmmm…Mmmm good!

God takes life's ingredients, most of which seem unpalatable, and He puts them into His big blender. In goes sickness, political tension, personal disappointment, financial strains, relational challenges, and fears hidden within the soul. Out from God's blender comes surprising blessings! More than palatable, with God's blender at work, all things turn out Mmmm … Mmmm good!

Does it seem like some life events taste good and others are bitter? Does it seem like there is no pattern to experiences in different areas of your life, as though the parts of your life are disconnected from each other? Does it feel like some past events can't be rewound, and are still conspiring against you today, over-ruling any good?

The word symphony means the combining of individual sounds toward one beautifully flowing piece of music. The individual sounds of instruments warming up all at the same time is almost intolerable. Then the conductor walks out. The instruments become quiet. The conductor lifts the baton while the musicians follow his orchestration. Beautiful music streams forth.

When you just stop and try to quietly take inventory of your life, does your life still seem like just a bunch of noise? Watch God orchestrate together the noisy pieces of your life into a beautiful symphony. Though there are events and people we may have *assumed* to be working against us, for those who love Him and have said "yes" to His redirecting call, God takes those very events and people and orchestrates them all together for good.

You are God's personal work project! Whenever you are tempted to turn...

    ... bitter about how your life has turned out

    ... regretful about past blunders

    ... cynical about your future

    ... distrustful of others

just remember that God is mixing into His blender every single thing in your life so that it will all come together as good for you. When events and people appear to be against you, anticipate God proving that it will all turn out *for* you.

Are there noisy parts of your life that sound off key to you? Are you resisting the very instruments in your life that God wants to blend into a symphony?

Live as though God is leveraging your life toward good.

"All things *work* together for the good…"

Romans 8:28 HCSB

When humans are at work, individually or collectively, you never can know for sure if the result is going to be good or bad. But when God is at work, the result is always good.

The word "work" carries with it the idea of leverage. When *you* work to bring good into your life, it's like trying to lift a 4,000-pound vehicle by bending down and grabbing the bottom of it with your own arms. You don't get much if any lift. *God* bringing good into your life is much different. God's Divine work is leveraged, like inserting a car jack under the vehicle to make the lifting so much easier.

When it comes to investing, leveraging funds[14] is an extremely powerful method toward growth. When an item goes down, you buy, and when it goes down more, you buy more, and so forth until it starts to go back up. When it goes up to the price you first paid, your investment will not be worth merely what you paid. Its value will be much greater. Invest when things are down and the lift you enjoy later is astonishing.

When you are down, God invests in you, His child. Then when you go even lower in life, He invests even more

---

[14] Using debt as a form of financial leverage is not advisable.

of Himself into you. You value God in your life much more during the days when you are low. You become more filled with total dependency on God when you are down. He specializes in giving extra value to those who have been hit hard by life. Then as He lifts you up, you find you have become so much more enriched as compared to before. You become a more useful, fruit-bearing child of God. That's God's leveraging power at work in your life. Begin right now to live as though God is already leveraging your life toward good.

Joseph dreamed God-sized dreams, and his brothers threw him in a pit and left him for dead. Years later, his brothers encountered Joseph by surprise, and were completely shocked to see that he had become the vice-president of Egypt.

His brothers came hungry during famine. Joseph could have returned evil for evil, but instead, he knew that all things had truly worked out for the good because of His love for God. To the very brothers who tried to take his life, Joseph gave food which saved their lives. He told them that what they meant for evil, God used for good. (Genesis 50:20) Joseph being left for *dead* resulted in Joseph bringing *life* to thousands during a long famine.

No doubt evil is trying its hardest to rule the world. The dark threads of disease, violence, war, drugs, racism, riots, poverty, hopelessness and hurt attempt to weave themselves together into a rope that wants to strangle us. But God overrules all evil. God's overruling hand is mightily at work everywhere, all the time, turning bad into good for those who follow Him.

When I was born, my legs were not formed correctly. The hospital broke both my legs and put them in casts for several months. I'm sure I cried like a baby! Even so, during those months of pain and confinement, my leg muscles worked harder than if my legs had been normal.

Eventually, the casts were taken off. God must have grown super powered muscles into those little legs of mine, because I easily learned to walk on an Indonesian bound ship bouncing with the waves. Not even the brutal high seas could stop those powerful legs. Even now at sixty, my legs get into a natural stride after a mile and a half of swimming and make me feel as though the race has just begun. In God's hands, today's handicap is tomorrow's asset.

Life is often stormy. God sometimes chooses to miraculously calm the storm. When He works in that way, don't say, "My life is calm because I'm living right. I'm finally getting the good results of all my hard work and virtue." No. It's not *your* goodness that causes God to be at work. It's *His* goodness. He is at work calming the storm in your life. Don't act like you have the ability to calm the sea my friend!

Often, instead of calling the sea to be still, God chooses to steer us right through the turbulent waves raging all around us as He guides us toward home. When life is tough, trust. Trust Him to take those dark threads of evil storm clouds and weave them into His larger tapestry of glorious good. He is doing so right now for those who love Him and have said "yes" to His redirecting call.

Set your heart on His purpose for you.

For we know that all things work together for good

for those who are called according to His purpose.

Romans 8:28

We end this chapter where we began; with the question, "What is the good life?" Is the good life found when you become successful? Does life become good when you have learned to feel good about yourself? Does being rich and healthy make life good?[15] Are we supposed to determine a purpose for our lives, and in fulfilling that self-defined purpose enjoy a good feeling?

No, the good life does not come by pursuing our own purposes. The good life comes by discovering and fulfilling our Creator's purpose for each of us. Only the One who created us truly knows what is ultimately good for us. The Lord has one overarching purpose for all His children. The great promise of God working it all out for the good of those called to His purpose must be understood in the context of the very next verse:

For God ... chose them to

become like his Son...

Romans 8:29

---

[15] There is a difference between immediate good and ultimate good. God promises ultimate good, even out of what is immediately not good.

152

God's goodness is promised to those whose heart is surrendered to the life-transforming Christ. Life is good when we are being supernaturally changed by Christ. All things work for our good when our heart is set on allowing God's Spirit within us to make us more like Jesus.

Becoming more like Jesus through His power makes life good. The good life is being freed from self by Christ. Life is good when we no longer merely trudge forward through tough circumstances as best we can, but instead soar with the Higher purpose of glorifying God through Christlikeness. The Spirit-empowered Christ follower is fully alive to freely live the good life in the glorious likeness of Christ.

You ask, "But what if a true follower of Christ sins?" The child of God who strays from God will experience His loving correction, and in that be affirmed of the Father's goodness. If you have genuinely come under conviction about your sinful state, repented of sin, and come to Christ for salvation from sin, He has given you a full pardon. You cannot sin your way out of God's purpose because your sin is the very thing His saving purpose intentionally redeems.

Why does God not change our circumstances to bring immediate good to us? Though we pray for Him to change the situation, God is at work changing us. He is helping our eyes see His ultimate plan in the middle of our current circumstances. His ultimate plan is to change *us*.

What makes life good is not good circumstances, but a Christ-like interaction with our circumstances. The same sun that melts wax hardens clay. No matter how bad things get, if you have given self to God, then you know that God is using bad circumstances toward His good purpose of making you more like Christ.

Becoming like Christ means that we value what He values. We prayerfully discern our thoughts and conform our thoughts to the mind of Christ. We willingly allow the Spirit within to align the passions of our hearts with the passions of Christ. We embrace what He embraces and we abhor what He abhors. It's then that we are surprised by how *sweet* life is.

If you have not responded to God's call to live for Christ, you have not yet entered into His goodness. Without Christ as King of your heart you are left to view life's events as random chance, and you have no alternative but to just make the best of the hand "fate" dealt you.

The good life does not come by seeking it. It is a by-product of the life surrendered to the Lordship of Christ. Come to the cross where Jesus died so you can live. Your sin has blocked you from God's goodness. Jesus died to remove that blockage, but you must turn from the sin of living for self. Ask Him to forgive you and give you new life. Give yourself to Him. Then get ready, because you will taste the sweet goodness of God more than you could have imagined. In His goodness, you will really live at last.

Discussion Questions

1. What makes life good? How would many people define "the good life"?

2. Read Romans 8:28-29. Is this promise made by God to *all* mankind? If not, what are the qualifications for being able to claim this promise?

3. On a scale of 1 (low) to 10 (high), how confident are you in …

   _____ God's providence?
   _____ all life's events being orchestrated by God for good?
   _____ Disease, racial tension, and general unrest as all working toward God's plan?

4. Look at the 7 points of the outline.
   Which one is easiest for you?

   Which is most difficult?

5. Recall the story of Joseph's treatment by his brothers. Read Genesis 50:20. Any personal examples of things people meant for bad yet God used those things for good?

6. Read Romans 8:26-29. Contrast the "don't know" in verse twenty-six with the "know" in twenty-eight.

How is God's purpose in twenty-eight defined in twenty-nine?

7. The same sun that melts wax hardens clay. What makes life good is not good circumstances, but how the heart interacts with all circumstances. Though we pray for God to change circumstances, He is at work changing both our eyes so we can see His plan, and our hearts so we are willing to become more like Christ in the here and now. Write your prayer of response to God here:

For he knew all about us before we were born
and he destined us from the beginning
to share the likeness of his Son.
This means the Son is the oldest among a vast family of
brothers and sisters who will become just like him.
Having determined our destiny ahead of time,
he called us to himself
and transferred his perfect righteousness
to everyone he called.
And those who possess his perfect righteousness
he co-glorified with his Son!
Romans 8:29-30 TPT

Not a Do It Yourself Project!

Five Ways *God* Makes Us Fully Alive

For simple projects, a do-it-yourself approach usually works well. Painting a bedroom may be doable. Yet for more complex projects, you might not want to take a D-I-Y approach. Painting a soaring living room requiring thirty-foot-high scaffolding is probably not the wisest thing for an amateur to attempt.

The most complex project you and I face is the human soul. Your soul is not a project to tackle by yourself. Your soul was designed by God to love Him and enjoy Him forever. Something has happened to keep you from experiencing all that love and enjoyment. Your soul has been filled with things other than God, leaving Him crowded out.

You've become so accustomed and attached to the junk accumulating in your soul that you have no thought of getting rid of any of it. How do I know this to be true about you? Because it's true about me. It's true about all of us.

You and I hoard junk in our souls. A hoarder requires an intervention. The Lord waits on you to willingly allow His decluttering invasion of your soul. When you let Him, He will enter your core being, do the necessary hauling away, and make your simplified clean heart fit to be His home. No longer do you have to sort through stacks of stuff to figure out how to live. Through

Christ the clutter-buster, you will start becoming fully alive.

Wait. Most hoarders think they don't need such an intervention. Perhaps you are becoming aware of the need for a change of heart, but you think intervention is not required. You may be so focused on improving the condition of your soul by your own human effort that you're missing out on God's readiness to recreate you into someone who, like Christ, is supernaturally alive.

> Your soul was designed by God to love Him and enjoy Him forever.

Becoming fully alive is not just a de-cluttering project. The dilapidated human soul is a decaying hoarder home requiring nothing short of a bull dozer. The project requires tearing down and rebuilding: definitely not a D-I-Y kind of thing!

You are *God's* building project! God the *builder* drew up the plan in eternity past. On the cross, God the *giver* paid the price for building you. God the *cornerstone* wants to lay a new foundation on which to rebuild your life.

How can your life be rebuilt? First you must be done with your own blueprint for your life. It's time to let Him tear down the work you have done by self-effort. Throw away your sketchy plans. Turn instead to God the builder.

He will then begin *His* construction plan. God the *founder* lays His foundation and hangs a sign on you; "Under God's Construction." God the *faithful* keeps on building your life even when you want to quit. God the *finisher* will soon present you as His completed project.

It's an exhilarating experience to fly from east to west on an all-night flight. Everything you thought you understood about time gets challenged. Flying from Asia to America, you can actually arrive in the west before you left the East! That's because those living in the East are literally already living in the West's tomorrow.

There's something even more fascinating than the time travel associated with such a flight. You can actually experience the sun rising again and again and again as the plane curves around the earth's surface at sunrise in many time zones. You can see the horizon stretching both into the future ahead of you, where it is light, and into the past behind you, where it fades into remote darkness.

You are far above the clouds, with a rare perspective not only of where you came from but also of where you are going. It can seem as if you are suspended in an unreal world, actually traveling while time stands still for you. In fact, you are grasping a more real view of the world than you had before. On such a flight the taller mountains of the world actually peak through the clouds, marking your journey.

There are five ways in which God makes us fully alive. Think of these as five major mountain peaks marking your life's journey. Those who are fully alive are able to see life from God's higher perspective, past, present, and future all suspended in time as one, and it is exhilarating.

God knows His people before we become His people.

For God knew his people in advance…

160

Romans 8:29

This verse uses the word "know," which in the original language of the New Testament is *ginosko*. To "ginosko" someone is to have intimate, personal relationship with them. Yet this particular verse adds something unusual to the usual *ginosko*. This verse says that God *"pro-ginoskos"* us. The *pro* means in advance. Though it seems impossible, God had intimate, personal knowledge of you before you were born, before Christ came to earth, and even before the creation of the earth thousands of years ago!

He chose us in Christ before the creation of the world.[16] This marvelous foreknowledge is so mind-boggling, it caused one believer to sing of it. His song became one of the Psalms of the Bible. "You saw me before I was born. Every day of my life was recorded in your book. Every moment was laid out..."[17]

Stunning. God set His love on us back before time began. You and I have been on His heart for a very long time.

Are you troubled by the circumstances surrounding how you came to be? Be troubled no more! You were not a surprise baby. You were not an afterthought. You are not merely the result of perhaps unplanned sexual union. You are not a mistake. You are not merely someone whose birth mother may have been raped. *You are one God has been waiting to love for a long time.*

---

[16] Ephesians 1:4
[17] Psalm 139:16.

Repeat out loud: "I am someone God has been waiting to love for a long time." Let that sink in.

Do you find yourself striving to earn the attention or approval of others? You do not need to strive to earn God's love or attention. Your place in God's heart is *not* secured by what you have done for Him. It's all about *what He did for you* on the cross. You did not reach out to God first. He reached out to you. God initiated a relationship with you before time began.

> God has been waiting for an eternity just to love you.

Why do you continue living as if life is a do-it-yourself project? Why are you still insecure about your relationship with God? From His viewpoint, it is easy to see your past horizon; God has known and loved you from eternity past.

God predetermined His people to be those who willingly conform to Christ.

For God knew his people in advance,

and he chose them to become like his son...

Romans 8:29

The word translated as *chosen* is, in the original language *pro Horizo*. As we have already seen, putting *pro* before a Greek word means the action word attached to *pro* was done in advance. *Horizo* means to determine the limits, or boundaries. We get our word *horizon* from *horizo*. The horizon determines the boundaries of space. For God to "pro-horizo" something means that God determines in advance what the boundaries will be. God determined long ago that the boundary marker for being His child is the cross. Those in Christ are in-bounds, and those without Christ are out-of-bounds.

Before a 5K run, the organizers go through the course, carefully marking the boundaries to predetermine the limits of the course. They use paint on the road surface, arrows at the turns, and even post people along the way to guide the runners.

God is the organizer who has marked out in advance the path to relationship with Him. God has predetermined that the boundary line of His Kingdom allows into His Kingship those who willingly submit self to become like Christ.

God's people are not trying to become like other people in this world. Christ followers are being conformed by God day by day to be more like Jesus. When verse thirty talks about Him calling us to come to Christ, it uses the root word for our word "morph." God morphs us into the shape of Christ. He is causing us to willingly conform to the shape of Christ.

How does God mold us into the image of Christ? There are many ways. One primary method is circumstances. The very situation we ask God to change may be the very thing He uses to change us into Christlikeness. Our destiny is to first become God's children, then become like Jesus. God can and does use any circumstances, good or bad, to move us toward our destiny.

Our destiny has less to do with *what we do* than it does *who we imitate*. Whose applause do you seek? Live for the applause of nail scarred hands.

Develop the lost passions of Christ. How do we develop a heart of passion for what moved our Lord? What should we value most? How should we live?

Live for the Kingdom. Thirst for intimacy with the Father. Hunger more for communion with the Creator than for food. Be deeply burdened for those who don't know Christ. Seek to walk moment by moment in step with the Spirit.

What if you had all the money you would ever need and you knew you couldn't fail at whatever you attempted? What passion would you pursue?

Your answer to that question is your life's purpose. Your passion should go beyond the choice of a vocation to arrive at your life purpose.

Regardless of your vocational pursuit, I dare you to live for the consuming passion of becoming like Christ.

It's then you find yourself fulfilling your destiny.

> God is on the move forward, showing you new horizons.

What, at this moment, is your consuming passion?

The horizon is a line at which the earth's surface and the sky appear to meet. In an airplane, the horizon goes on and on beyond what we can clearly make out.

When you move forward with the plane, the horizon opens up into new spaces you had not seen even a split second before. Move toward the horizon, and new horizons keep appearing.

God reveals more and more of Himself to you each day you venture a little further forward in being morphed into Christlikeness. Don't settle for landing the plane and being content with only spiritual memories of the good ol' days. God is on the move forward, showing you new horizons. Venture into the horizon in front of you, and you will experience the life God marked out, predestined for you long ago. Which way are you looking: backward to what was, or forward to God's new horizon for you?[18]

God calls His people to separate themselves.

And having Chosen them,

he called them to come to him.

And having called them,

he gave them right standing with himself.

And having given them right standing,

he gave them his glory.

Romans 8:30

---

[18] I recommend David Jeremiah's book *Forward*.

Before time began, we were chosen to be loved with an everlasting love. We were predestined to conform to Christ. Yet we live in the now. In this life of ours today, we live in right standing with God, as His separate people. In the future, we will be glorified with Him for eternity.

When God calls us, He does so while we are still in the midst of the world's ways. If we say yes to His call, then we leave the ways of this world, and go with God and His people on a different path.

On an old TV show, Bob Barker would call a name from the studio audience, while he said, "Come on down. You are the next contestant on *The Price is Right*." The called person would excitedly separate themselves from the crowd to come be with the Master of Ceremonies. You and I have heard our names called by God, and have gladly separated ourselves from the crowd to be with the Master.

He calls you by name! He stirs your heart to respond to His love. "Matthew, wake up to my love. Come away with me."

"But God, I'm not qualified."

"I didn't ask for your resume. I asked for your heart."

"I need to clean up before I can come to you."

"I do the cleaning. Just come."

God doesn't call qualified people. He qualifies the called. He calls people...

out of death and into life

out of sin and into holiness

out of Satan's darkness into God's light

out of earth's gravitational pull into flying high across God's horizon

out of religion and into relationship

out of striving and into the security of grace

out of isolation and into community.

Paul wrote to believers in Rome where Emperor Nero made sport out of persecuting Christ followers. Paul wrote to people whose friends walked into the famous Roman coliseum singing praise songs while the crowds cheered and the lions devoured them. When God calls, the call is a calling away from doing as you please. It is a call to suffer with Christ.[19]

God calls you now. Have you said yes? Or have you ignored His call? Say yes! Come out from the crowd and be with the Master. Say yes to God, and become fully alive, even while living surrounded by danger.

God gives those in Christ right standing with Him.

And having called them,

he gave them right standing with himself.

Romans 8:30

---

[19] See Philippians 1:29

You are under a heavy load of sin that you cannot remove. When you ask God, He transfers the load from you to Christ on the cross. He declares you "pardoned." He can do so because He substituted Himself in your place as He paid with His own blood the penalty you should have paid.

The word righteousness means to acquit in a legal sense. God's love for you is so great He is willing to pay the highest possible price for you. You were sentenced to death because you lived for self instead of for your Creator. But God let Jesus die in your place. God did everything it took to make it possible for you to be with Him. Those who have come to Christ stand before Holy God without the shame of sin, without the guilt of sin, and without the separation from God brought on by sin.

Do you have a right standing with God through Christ?

God gives us His glory.

And having given them right standing,

He gave them his glory.

Romans 8:30

The word "glory" is the word *doxa*, from which we get our word doxology. It means to ascribe weight, or to reveal the true value of something. To have glory is to not be taken lightly, but to be given much weighty consideration.

What does being glorified mean? When you give your life to Christ, He gives you His glory, His supernatural nature. Your soul becomes super-naturalized. You shine with the light of Christ. You are God's bling! Your face beams with the likeness of Jesus Himself.

One day soon, you will be raised from this earth and given a glorified body. (I Cor. 15:36,42) You will be taken into His eternal Kingdom (John 17:24). Your works will be rewarded (Revelation 3:21, 22:12). You will be given a realm of reign with Christ (I Cor. 6:2-3, Romans 8:17).

Those He knew in advance He predestined. Those He predestined He called. Those He called He made right with Himself. Those He made right with Himself He glorifies.

So much for the do-it-yourself approach of trying to come to God on your own effort. Though your reactive cooperation is needed, every part of the work required to make you fully alive is initiated by our proactive God. Worship the One eternally at work transforming us from sinners into reflections of His glory!

Discussion Questions

1. Which of the following best describes your spiritual life?

   _____ Trying to build it up, but like most DIY projects, there are delays.

   _____ Working hard to do the right things

   _____ Finding that I make promises to God and self, then don't keep them.

   _____ Just letting go of any responsibility and letting God.

   _____ Submitted to Christ, seeking to responsibly do His will alone in His power alone, following His plan for me.

2. Read Romans 8:29-30. What are the five verbs? Who is the one doing the action of each verb? In what ways are we, in response to God's work, responsible in partnering with Him in each of these 5 areas?

Five Verbs	The One Doing the Work	Our Response

3. Which of the five actions of God make you feel the most treasured by Him? Why?

4. *ProHorizo* means to pre-determine the limits of something, to mark-out beforehand. Predestination means that God has predetermined the boundary line of His Kingdom to be those who willingly submit self to become like Christ.
How does this Biblical definition of predestination clear up extra-Biblical concepts about predestination?

5. Romans 8:30 says God called us. The word "call" is the same New Testament word as "church", which describes the assembly of those called out by God. Which of the following is true?

   ____ God calls qualified people.
   ____ God qualifies called people.

   In what ways do you see that you are God's building project? In what areas is He renovating your life now, calling you to be set apart from the common ways of the world around us?

6. If money were no object and you knew you couldn't fail, what passion would you pursue?

7. Extra Credit: Look up the following verses and note in each verse the particular way God will glorify us in the future.

1 Corinthians 15:36,42

_____

_____

John 17:24

_____

_____

Revelation 3:21, 22:12

_____

_____

1 Corinthians 6:2-3

_____

_____

Romans 8:17

_____

_____

So what does all this mean? If God has determined to stand with us, tell me, who then could ever stand against us? For God has proved his love by giving us his greatest treasure, the gift of his Son. And since God freely offered him up as the sacrifice for us all, he certainly won't withhold from us anything else he has to give. Who then would dare to accuse those whom God has chosen in love to be his? God himself is the judge who has issued his final verdict over them—"Not guilty!"

Who then is left to condemn us? Certainly not Jesus, the Anointed One! For he gave his life for us, and even more than that, he has conquered death and is now risen, exalted, and enthroned by God at his right hand. So how could he possibly condemn us since he is continually praying for our triumph? …

All day long we face death threats for your sake, God. We are considered to be nothing more than sheep to be slaughtered! Yet even in the midst of all these things, we triumph over them all, for God has made us to be more than conquerors, and his demonstrated love is our glorious victory over everything!

Romans 8:31-34, 35-37 TPT

More than Conquerors!

Ahn Ai Kim was only a middle school student when the Japanese invaded and conquered Korea. The Japanese forced all Koreans to bow in worship to the Japanese Shinto shrine. Ahn Ai was a follower of Christ, and though many Christ followers bowed their knees as ordered, she refused to bow to the ground before anyone other than the One True God.

Student groups arrived from all the area schools to bow in worship before a man-made object. Ahn Ai's group was the last to arrive. She looked around, and saw that every single person was bowing before the Shinto idol. She uttered to herself the words spoken by Esther in the Old Testament, who dared to take an unpopular stand before her ruler. "If I perish, I perish." She then prayed. "Lord, I die to self. You, Christ my Lord, live in me and through me."

A commanding Japanese voice interrupted her prayer. *"Gwanshim! Hwal!"* "Attention! Bow!"

Everyone bowed their knees and bent their bodies low to the ground, thrusting themselves forward toward the shrine as a symbol of full surrender to the god Shinto. Only one stood alone; Ahn Ai Kim, who became known as Esther Kim.

On the way back to the school building, none of Esther's friends spoke to her. Everyone was very uncomfortable even being near her, so they hurried ahead of her into the building. When Esther arrived near the building, she saw four Japanese policemen waiting outside. Esther fled before being noticed, and lived in hiding for months. During those lonely days, she prepared to go to prison, knowing she had to eventually go back to school and stand before the shrine once again. To ready herself for capture and torture, she memorized chapters of the Bible and scripture songs. She ate out of the garbage to toughen up her digestive system, and she fasted.

God called Esther out of hiding to stand for Him. As a result, she spent six years in prison. Just as she had before, she boldly proclaimed allegiance to God alone. Esther suffered much brutality, but never retaliated. Instead she showed sacrificial love for her enemies and for other prisoners. Through Esther Kim's powerful influence, many prisoners and even some of the Japanese invaders placed their faith in Christ. During the six years of torture in confinement Esther felt closer to the Lord.

Esther's feelings and experiences are similar to the situation we find in Romans chapter eight. As Paul wrote these uplifting words of wonderful encouragement to the believers in Rome, he likely reflected on how he had been lashed with a whip, beaten with a metal rod, stoned and left for dead, shipwrecked, accused falsely, and imprisoned for five years.

No doubt, Paul thought about the believers in Rome. There the Emperor was making a sport out of harassing Christ followers, hanging them on crosses, and burning them alive. To those suffering under such cruelty, Paul had the audacity to say to them, "You are more than conquerors!"

You would think people like Esther Kim and the apostle Paul would be bitter due to unfair treatment. How remarkable that instead we see in them only boldness, confidence, winsomeness, and an unbeatable spirit.

That's the way I want to be in these troubling times. How about you? How is such an approach to life's difficulties even possible?

Though the accuser seeks to guilt us, God is *for us*.

Though some would attempt to condemn us, God chose *us*.

Though the enemy tries to defeat us, in Christ we are more than conquerors.

Christ died *for us*. He rose again *for us*. Christ now pleads *for us*. Christ loves *us* through thick and thin. If you

> Life is rigged; It's rigged by God to work in your favor.

and I have died to self to be raised to new life in Christ, we are **unbeatable**!

Have you given your life in surrender to the will of Christ? Then He is *for you*. He has already rigged life to work in your favor. He makes you unstoppable. Here's a math formula that will forever change the bottom line equation of your life. Insert your name in place of mine in this truth:

J. Matthew Nance + God = Enough	(Your Name) _____ + God = Enough

Worried about losing life's battles?   God is for you! Who can win against Him?

What shall we say about such wonderful things as these?

If God is for us, who can ever be against us?

Since He did not spare even his own Son

but gave him up for us all,

won't he also give us everything else?

Romans 8:31-32

In the beginning, God created us in His image. Since then we've been creating God in our image, reducing the Almighty into idols much like us. A. W. Tozer said that we tend to reinvent Him as a god who can never surprise us, never overwhelm us, nor astonish us, nor transcend us. Tozer prayed that the hammer of the high God would smash our small mindedness.

The God of the Bible is all powerful. The One True God is all knowing. He is all present. The Lord is high and exalted above all. He does more than we could ever ask or even imagine.

His *thoughts* are way higher than my thoughts.

His *ways* are incomparably higher than mine.

I don't control His *power.*

I don't understand His *mind.*

I don't deserve His *mercy.*

He is *more than able* for every battle before me.

How do we know God is for us? Do we know God is favoring us if the crowd at our place of worship is growing in comparison to other houses of worship? Is He on our side in the same way we pray before a football game, asking God to help our team win instead of the other team?

If we never encounter difficulty or opposition, does that mean God has favored us? Is an increase in material "blessings" a sign of God's smile? We want to imagine all these things as signals of God's favor. And there are many people who claim to speak for God today who would have you believe in a health and prosperity "gospel."

If God's favor is found in popularity, material gain, and lack of opposition, then Jesus was out of God's favor for much of His life. The closer He walked toward the cross, the more the crowd around Him shrank. Jesus gained nothing materially that could point toward God's "blessing," and He faced constant opposition. Despite not having any of these popular signs of God's supposed "favor," God the Son was highly favored by God the Father.

Look again at Romans 8:32. How do we know God is for us? Because He did not spare even His own for us. He spared no expense in bringing us into His great heart of love. The cross is how we know God is irreversibly for us.

Since God is for us, who can be against us? Actually, lots of people *can* and likely *will* be against us, but what does it matter?

What enemies are trying to defeat you right now? Have you been deceived into seeing the challenges of your life as giants who can crush you instead of seeing yourself as more than a conqueror? Is life getting the best of you? Your Father is a big strong King. He gives His power to even the scrawniest of His kids.

Satan is against Christ followers, but his power is puny compared to Christ. All those influenced by evil may be against us, but they are on a very short leash in God's hand. Rivals may envy us and seek to out-position us, but in the end God and God's people win. God orchestrates all of life toward the good for those who love Him and have said "yes" to His redirecting call.

Christ was "delivered up." Someone gave Jesus up to be killed. Who delivered Him up?

Did Judas deliver Him up for money?

Did Pilate deliver Him up out of fear?

Did the Jews deliver Him up because of envy?

Did the soldiers deliver Him up for a promotion?

No. They were all, without realizing it, just helping God to do His thing. *God* delivered up His son because of love.

God loves us so much that He gave the greatest love gift ever. He gave His prized and only Son to die for us. What great love!

Do we prize Christ the way the Father does, as the greatest love gift ever?

Do we put greater value on a new car, a new relationship, a new career, or a new home more than we value God's love gift to us? Do we de-value Christ by our misplaced priorities? Is there a need for us to repent and come back to our first love?

Are we worried that life's enemies will keep our needs from being met? Do we fear that a disaster will take away our homes? Are we afraid a disease will wipe us out?

Since He did not spare even his own Son but delivered Him up for us all, won't he also give us all things? "No eye has seen, no ear has heard, and no mind has imagined what God has prepared for those who love him." (I Corinthians 2:9)

Do you fear that God is unresponsive to your needs as His child? Since God may not act in your favor and within your time frame, *do you live as though you must fight your own battles?*

The war for God's favor has been won already on the cross. The battle has already been won. God has done what it takes to supply all your needs. He is more eager than you are to make sure you live fully supplied with what you truly need. If it seems He is unresponsive, perhaps you have yet to begin depending on Him.

Have you placed your life under the Lordship of Christ? If you have, victory and the favor of the King of

Kings have already been secured. He conquered the enemy, making you more than a conqueror through Him. As more than a conqueror, you don't have to fight life's battles on your own. God gives all things to you because you have said yes to the greatest love gift ever offered.

Are you worried about losing life's battles? God is for you! Who can win against Him? Your biggest battle has already been won on the cross. Live like the conqueror you are!

Feeling guilty until proven innocent? God has ruled you to be righteous. Who can over-rule Him?

Who dares accuse us whom God has chosen for his own?

No one - for God himself has given us

right standing with himself.

Romans 8:33

Who can accuse you? No doubt, there are many who can and do attack you with false accusations. Sometimes you may be accused about things in which, though you are guilty, you have already sought and received the forgiveness of both God and man. The accuser is relentless in digging up the dirt of your imperfect past and throwing it in your face. The enemy of your soul will speak condemnation into your heart and mind over and over like a recording on an endless playback loop.

Accusation may come from your own conscience working overtime in sync with the devil. You may have "friends" who show up to "pray for you," and out of a sense of power over you, enjoy serving as your tour guide on guilt trips. Are you tortured by false and even true accusations from the enemy? Remember this: On judgment day, other believers will not be able to bring a charge against you. Neither the angels nor the demons will be able to declare you guilty of anything. Even Satan himself won't have a single word of accusation against you.

You will stand before One and only One Judge over your life: your Creator. The Judge has already declared that all those who have come to the cross of Christ are acquitted from all charges. The guilt price was paid by the blood of Christ. All those whom God justifies are safe from accusation.

What will you say next time you hear accusing voices inside your head?

"You'll never be good enough." Say, "*God* has ruled me to be righteous. You can't overrule Him."

"Why would anyone even care about the likes of you?" Say, "God has ruled me righteous. *You* can't overrule Him."

"How can you live with yourself after what you've done?" Say, "God has ruled me *righteous*. You can't overrule Him."

"Everyone knows the hidden you. Your secret is out." Say, "God has ruled me righteous. You *can't overrule* Him."

"And you think God is going to accept the likes of you in the condition you're in?" Say, "God has ruled me righteous. You can't overrule *Him*."

"Self, who am I trying to fool? I am not worthy of God chasing after me." Say, "God has ruled me righteous. *I* can't overrule Him."

> Live like the conqueror you are!

To become justified by God, agree with God that you have lived for self, and have ignored the One who created you for relationship with Him. Turn from sin and self toward Him. Ask His forgiveness through death to self with Christ on the cross. Receive new life through Christ's resurrection. The Lord will clear your record and change your standing before Him from guilty to righteous.

Have you come to the cross to get right with God? If not, is there anything that would keep you from getting right with God now? Seek a Christ following friend to help you do so. If you are right with God through the blood of Christ, you can confidently say, "I am justified by God. It is just-as-if-I'd never sinned." Live like the conqueror you are!

Trying to prove yourself to others? God gave His all for you on the cross. Who can devalue you?

Who then will condemn us?

No one- for Christ Jesus died for us

and was raised to life for us,

and he is sitting in the place of honor

at God's right hand, pleading for us.

Romans 8:34

Humans in general are much like crabs in a basket. Fishermen know you don't need a lid for a basket of crabs. When one crabs start to climb out, the other crabs pinch him and pull him down. We are crabby by nature, pulling down the value of each other. We are even prone to devalue our own souls and sell ourselves to the lowest bidder. Pretty soon, we start believing that we belong at the bottom of a stinky, crabby basket.

The value of something in the marketplace is determined by what someone is willing to pay for it. If there is consistently high demand and people are waiting in line willing to pay above asking price, the price will inevitably go up. If no one values something enough to pay the asking price, the price will inevitably go down.

The marketplace has become crowded with posters trying to boost value. To increase our perceived value, we post social network pieces to bring esteem our direction. To present ourselves in the best light possible, we spin each and every story in such a way that self always comes out looking good. We work in vain to prove our own worth to others and to self. *Our value does not lie in who we are but in Whose we are.* One clue to value of something is the place where the thing was made. Who claims to be the originator of the item?

He left His glorious mansion and came as a man into our dusty streets, walking in our market stamping his

"Made in Heaven by My love" stamp on every human life. Suddenly, everything changed.

Left to the street market value, our lives might not bring a very high price in the sight of ourselves or others. And yet Someone has shown up at the market of humanity with very deep pockets, paying an extremely high price and driving up the value of every single human being.

What price was God willing to pay for you? He spared no expense. He gave the only Son He had for you. God the Father let God the Son be made a curse, be spit on, whipped, and crucified, all for you. When the Son took on the sin of humanity on the cross, the Holy Father forsook His Own Son so *you* would never need to be God-forsaken.

Three days later, Jesus rose from the dead, giving His followers supernatural resurrection power to be more than conquerors. He is now at the right hand of God the Father. *He is at the Father's side to be on your side.*

Do you feel like the market forces around your life are driving the value of your life up or down, as if your life is a bobbing boat on a stormy sea? You must not live by that feeling. Drop an anchor from your soul down to the foundational, rock solid truth and steady your life on this ultimate reality; *nothing can undo what Jesus has done for you.*

Made in Heaven by My Love

God gave His all for you on the cross. You are of great value to Him. Who can devalue you? No one. So live like the conqueror you are.

In what ways are you being accused? In what ways is there an attack on the true value God has placed on you? Are you taking these distortions of reality to God and letting Him renew your mind on the basis of His truth instead of the accuser's lies?

Insecure about God's view of you? God's love beats all odds. What can separate you from Him?

Who shall separate us from the love of Christ?

Shall tribulation, or distress, or persecution,

or famine, or nakedness, or danger, or sword?

As it is written,

"For your sake we are being killed all the day long;

we are regarded as sheep to be slaughtered."

No, in all these things

we are more than conquerors through him who loved us.

Romans 8:35-37 ESV

A child who has been taken away from his or her parents often has separation anxiety, living with a continual fear that whenever he or she becomes close to someone, that person also may be taken away. Most all of us have experienced the loss of someone close to us, and we have some lingering separation anxiety.

While human relationships these days may seem disposable, God never abandons His child. He will never leave you. He will never forsake you. He will never give up on you.

Will there ever come a day when you as his child have messed up so bad that He says, "I'm fed up with you. The deal is off"? No. Never. The "deal" is that He has irrevocably given His undeserved favor to those who have said "yes" to His redirecting call of love through His son Christ Jesus from the cross. The "deal" is a permanent one. *There is no experience you may have that will rip you from God's strong arms of love.*

Not end time calamities

Not the pressures of life

Not persecution from following Christ

Not intense prolonged hunger

Not exposure to the elements

Not physical risk

Not violence

Not disaster, disease, or death itself

Does this mean the follower of Christ will not have difficulties? The opposite is true. We should expect difficulty as normal. Going with Christ often causes us to be counter-cultural. You can expect the forces of evil to come against someone who is doing good in the name of Christ. We are like sheep to be slaughtered. *Are you prepared to give up everything for Christ's sake?* Count the cost.

Each Christ follower is a part of His body. He will not allow any of us to be amputated. We may be weathered by life's storms, ridiculed and accused by Christ's enemies, and inflicted by physical challenges, but none of that takes us away from Christ. All of that draws us closer to Christ as we depend on Him for strength.

As he wrote the believers in Rome, Paul was pouring out his life for others for Christ's sake. Notice he says, "for your sake we are killed every day…" That's how we should live. May you and I die to self, being conformed with Him in His death. May we give ourselves fully, investing our lives into the lives of others for an eternal difference in God's Kingdom.

If we actually live that way, there may be times when we develop a martyr's complex. Even those who have grown spiritually to the point where they may go for days at a time not even giving much thought to self may suddenly start thinking, "What am I doing wasting my life on others? Poor, pitiful me. I've poured out all the love there is to give." No. God's love keeps pouring Himself into the soul of one who pours out all of self in Christ's love toward others.

> God's love keeps pouring into the one who pours out Christ's love to others.

In a life of giving self to others for Christ's sake, we are never removed from God's love. We are more than conquerors! In trials, we don't lose. We gain holiness, courage, and influence. Live like the conqueror you are!

In fact, we are more than conquerors. Romans 8:37 says, "we are more than conquerors through him who loved us." In the original language of the New Testament the wording for *more than conquerors* is *uper nikao*. This is the only place in the entire New Testament where these words are used together.

From *uper* we get our words *uber* and hyper, both words pointing to something beyond ordinary. From *nikao* comes the word Nike, which mean victorious. Those experiencing the Father's love in Christ are *uber nike*; super conquerors, overwhelmingly victorious, hyper triumphant.

God is for you.

God chose you.

Christ died for you.

Christ rose again for you.

Christ pleads for you.

Christ loves you.

So live fully alive, because in Christ, you are more than a conqueror.

Discussion Questions

1. Which of the following most describes you? Which least describes you?

___ worried about losing life's battles

___ feeling guilty until proven innocent

___ trying to prove self to others

___ insecure about God's view of me

___ starting to taste God's goodness toward me

___ often enjoying being more than a conqueror

2. Read Romans 8:31-37. In what ways lately do you find yourself enrolled in the University of Hard Knocks? What is the closest you've come to feeling the despair and loneliness of being separated from God as described in these verses?

3. Memorize 1 Corinthians 2:9 by saying it out loud until you can do so without looking at the words, then repeat it five times, including the reference. During the past week, if you would have had that verse hidden in your heart, what specific situations would have had different outcomes because of your positive Biblical outlook?

How will you take the verse with you into the week ahead?

4. Read Romans 8:33-34 in several translations. In what ways have you been or are you being falsely accused?

In what ways is there an attack on the true value God has placed on you?

Are you taking these distortions of reality to God and letting Him develop your mind on the basis of His truth instead of the accuser's lies?

5. Read Romans 8:35-37. Paul was pouring out his life for others, for Christ's sake. That's how we should live. In all the self-sacrifice for Christ, we are more than conquerors! Even in trials, we still keep all we have and gain holiness, happiness, courage, and influence. Live like the conqueror you are! Write your response here as a prayer to God:

6. Extra Credit: Google "How did the 12 apostles die?" and compare your suffering to theirs.

Who could ever divorce us from the endless love of

God's Anointed One? *Absolutely no one!* For nothing in the

universe has the power to diminish his love toward us.

Troubles, pressures, and problems are unable to come

between us and heaven's love. What about persecutions,

deprivations, dangers, and death threats?

No, for they are all impotent to hinder omnipotent

love, even though it is written:

All day long we face death threats for your sake, God.

We are considered to be nothing more

than sheep to be slaughtered!

Yet even in the midst of all these things, we triumph over

them all, for God has made us to be more than

conquerors, and his demonstrated love is our glorious

victory over everything!

Romans 8:35-37 TPT

Impotent to Hinder
Omnipotent Love

Though I feel God's love when He comforts me, I feel His love the strongest when I suffer for Christ's sake. The enemy uses the suffering to attempt to pull God's love away from me. Why does God allow suffering in my life as a result of obediently following Christ? I may not why until I see Him face to face, but for now one thing is clear. When following Christ results in tough times, it causes me to depend even more on God's reassuring love.

Suffering doesn't have the power to pull God's child away from God's all-powerful love. In one verse, Romans points to seven possible negative results from following Christ, none of which are able to hinder God's love.

> Who shall separate us
> from the love of Christ?
> Shall tribulation, or distress, or persecution,
> or famine, or nakedness, or peril, or sword?
> Romans 8:35 NKJV

Nothing can separate God's child from His love. Though these seven forms of suffering for Christ are seldom experienced by western believers, Christ followers in many parts of the world today are quite familiar with fellowshipping with Christ in His sufferings. Such fellowship brings purity to God's people. Believers who suffer for the Kingdom develop a maturity that doesn't come as easily to believers who don't experience persecution. When you suffer for Christ, you become more connected with Him and His love.

If you have yet to experience spiritual opposition while following Christ, get ready. The Lord may be about to bless comfortable Christians around the world with suffering. In the past, American and European cultures were to a large degree "Christian." Now there are few places in the world where the Christian life is a cultural norm. Living for Christ in today's world is becoming more difficult. Are you ready and willing to face tribulation, distress, persecution, famine, nakedness, peril or sword for Christ's sake?

Jesus said that if you suffer for the Kingdom's sake, you are blessed. How could suffering possibly be a blessing? Once you suffer for Christ's sake, you will know His love for you like never before. You may think of being "blessed" as having a nice place to live, a good job, and other creature comforts. Jesus says "blessed" is what you are if you live for the next life- the Kingdom of God- even if it results in being mistreated in this life.

Are you a Christ follower? You are to live as the light of Christ pushing back the darkness of the world. You are to be a soldier marching to the gates of hell and unleashing God's barrier-busting, captive-releasing love.

There, on the battlefront His omnipotent love within you conquers the impotent enemy. There, the Lord purifies His bride the church and loves her passionately. There, as you suffer for Christ, you are strangely blessed.

Let's take a look at seven forms of suffering for the Lord that have no power to remove God's love from us.

*

After twelve years in Korea, God called us to serve in a large communist country of East Asia. Everywhere I went people somehow knew I was coming. Every taxi driver knew where to take me home without asking. Neighbors knew I was coming up the apartment steps before I got to the steps. Banking transactions were traced. In seemingly casual conversation, locals asked me questions about my activities. The most random people would talk to me about things they could have only known by my cell phone having been bugged. Our apartment was bugged as well. I began to realize none of this was by accident. I lived hemmed in.

In the country where we were called to live, gathering information on foreigners was profitable. The communist government paid sixty dollars for every piece of helpful information given them about foreigners. In those days, sixty dollars would have fed your family for two weeks.

There were more than 80,000 internet policemen. They quietly focused attention on the emails, log-ins, social media posts, searches, and blogs of foreigners like me. A VPN[20] did not provide complete protection.

Even those I considered friends would seek to gain income from relating to me. I noticed faces of people who never engaged me in conversation, yet were stalking me. Some chased me simply for the money they would be given once they gave their report. Others hunted me in hopes of bringing me harm and putting an end to the "spread of spiritual pollution." It became difficult to know who to trust.

Yet as a Christ follower I was to take the gospel entrusted to me and entrust it to others as I trained them to share the good news of Jesus. While attempting to remain cautious, I obediently shared the message of Christ and trained the new believers to start and lead their own simple house churches.

The target city was blanketed with thousands of gift-wrapped Luke and Acts scripture booklets, which also contained simple lessons to help new believers share their faith and start new groups. Several mass seed sowing projects resulted in hundreds of new believers and twenty or so new house churches.

The communist government was anxious about any gatherings not under their control. They cringed whenever non-government groups would share any information with people without government approval first. The authorities wanted to put an end to the beginnings of new churches.

They mistakenly thought that if they could remove the leader, they could destroy the movement. So they were constantly infiltrating our gatherings trying to figure out who the leader was and what was the leader's support network.

---

[20] Encrypted virtual private network

The truth was *every* believer was trained as a leader and was expected to bring people to faith in Christ and help form new house churches. The moles in house gatherings asked, "Who is the leader here?" The people would always look around at each other and reply, "We all are, but actually Jesus Christ is the head. We are His body." Christ followers may be decapitated, but Christ remains the head of His church.

Once moles could not determine who the leaders were, co-workers in the target city were being taken in by authorities and questioned. Some were not released quickly. Eventually authorities made connections back to me. Fortunately, I was informed that the interrogators were on the way to pick me up. My advisor told me to go to the airport and get on an international flight. A quick decision was made for Cheryl and the boys to not leave, but to stay put in our apartment until the end of the school year.

I was involuntarily a country away from my family for four long months. Even in a neighboring country, I still had to be careful about trusting others. The internet had made the world a small place.

My passport was blocked from re-entry. I felt hemmed out, like I was banished to a life of solitude on a remote island. Meanwhile Cheryl and the boys faced even more difficulty than I did.

Through the tribulation, I initially felt forsaken by God and was asking God "Why?" Then a friend named Merrill, who I sought out during exile pointed me to Jesus. Merrill said Jesus also felt forsaken by God and asked "Why?" Merrill asked me what Jesus said next from the cross.

Into your hands I commit my spirit.

After much silence, I began to weep. My anger toward God instantly turned into repentance for having become self-centered. I had demanded I be with my family in my home living my life the way I wanted. I went to my knees.

Lord, I commit my spirit into Your hands.

Then I began singing with deep emotion, "All to Jesus I surrender..." I had a death of self and a reboot into life for Christ's sake alone. I've never been the same since.

What would be your reaction if you were to face serious tribulation? The Bible says that to you it is given not only to believe on Him but to suffer for His sake.[21] Do you consider suffering for Christ to be normal? Or do you demand a persecution-free society?

*

Distress
Στενοχωρία *stenochória*

Internal tension
sense of pressure, anguish

While I was not able to come back home to the family, Cheryl found herself under house arrest. Two guards were posted outside the door of

---

[21] Philippians 1:29

our apartment all day and all night.

If Cheryl got on her bike to go buy groceries, one of the guards went with her on a bike. To feed our two teenage boys, she had to strap groceries every which way onto her bike. Eventually, Cheryl started telling the guard, "Since you are here at the store with me, you might as well strap some of the groceries onto your bike too."

At first, all of the guards were nice and helpful. They made the most apologetic excuses for coming in our apartment to search for spiritual propaganda, set up remote access into our computer, and plant listening devices around the house.

The apartment above has had a water leak.

There is a problem with your internet connection. It won't take long to fix it on your computer.

Rumor had it that I had somehow come back home briefly and they had missed me. That infuriated the authorities. They switched to a different set of guards who were much stricter and could not be bribed by Cheryl's chocolate chip cookies.

She lived hemmed in. The protocol between workers required those under surveillance to protect each other by making no contact at all. Neither Cheryl or the boys were allowed to associate with other foreigners. Even stopping to speak to each other on the street would have put the other workers under scrutiny.

Nothing could be said about our situation to anyone. For someone with the gift of hospitality like Cheryl, isolation was a harsh punishment. We had a local house helper whom Cheryl leaned on during house arrest, yet

200

even she was taken away, interrogated, and not allowed to come back.

During the four months of house arrest, while the boys rode their bikes home from school every day they may have wondered if their mother would still be there when they got home. What would they do if she had been taken away? The constant threat wore Cheryl down to total dependence on God like never before. It's still difficult for her to talk about the experience. Yet the Lord made it possible for her, even during distress, to provide a sense of safety and security for the boys.

Sometimes do you feel that following Christ has brought into your life more trouble than its worth? The enemy wants your suffering for Jesus to cause anxiety within you. Have you ever stepped out in bold obedience to Christ, only to experience an anxious feeling?

*

Persecution

Διωγμός diógmos

chased as prey
hunted like an animal
punished with hostility

Brother Yun was traveling all over his native China training Chinese to take the gospel to the ends of the earth. He had gone years without rest, feeling a great sense of urgency in raising up Chinese lovers of Jesus to take the good news of Jesus to the ends of the earth. They called themselves an army of ants. Though some of them got stepped on and killed by the enemy, there were so many of them in the army that the enemy could not stomp on all of them.

Authorities had been chasing after Brother Yun for years. Finally, one day they captured their prey. Chinese police raided a training event, surrounded Brother Yun, arrested him, and took him to prison. He felt like an eagle suddenly put in a cage. Yet God made it clear that He was giving Brother Yun a season of needed rest.

Brother Yun took the rest as an opportunity to fast and pray for all the men in the prison who needed Jesus. After a month of fasting, the prison guards began betting with each other on whether or not Brother Yun would live through the day.

The prison leaders tortured Brother Yun by shooting painful acid under his finger and toe nails, which caused him to faint. After 72 days of constant torture and taking in no food or water, authorities became convinced that Brother Yun was simply not going to die. Neither was he going to give them the names of his co-workers. He refused to be a second Judas.

After asking God to let him die but still not dying, Yun felt God was telling him to make disciples in the prison. Brother Yun was then put in charge of the death row criminals, including the murderers and rapists. He became the cell mate of a man known as Mad Dog, who bit his victims before killing them. Mad Dog wore a muzzle on his face to keep him from biting others. The muzzle also kept him from being able to eat well, so he was always hungry and angry.

God told Yun to give his own meager meals to Mad Dog. After arguing with God, he began to spoon feed his own food rations into the hole in Mad Dog's muzzle. In handcuffs and shackles, Mad Dog dropped to his knees weeping, saying, "Nobody loves me. Why do you?"

"Because Jesus loves you."

"Jesus? Who is He?"

"He is God, who loved you so much He came to this earth to die for you."

"I am to die in two days. What can Jesus do for me?

"He can save you from your sin and take you to live with Him forever in heaven."

"I need Jesus."

Brother Yun reached over and took the muzzle off Mad Dog's face. He didn't bite. Instead, in the middle of the night Mad Dog started singing, "I need Jesus." Soon all 800 prisoners joined him in singing, "I need Jesus."

Brother Yun spent four years in prison the first time, and was imprisoned two more times before being permanently banished from China. He continues training an army of ants today.[22]

What if you were to lead many people to believe in Jesus and disciple others, only to become chased as prey? What is God

---

[22] The Heavenly Man : The Remarkable True Story of Chinese Christian Brother Yun by Paul Hattaway, 2003.

saying to you through the true story of Brother Yun of China?

*

<table>
<tr><td>**Famine**
λιμός *limos*

hunger
scarcity of food</td><td>In 2009, forty-eight Christ followers lived in a village called Katin of Laos. They were told to stop following Jesus or they would suffer. Despite resistance from most neighbors and all authorities, they continued to worship and share their faith with others. One day they</td></tr>
</table>

watched as their animals were stolen, slaughtered and loaded up into vehicles. When the villagers continued to worship, authorities came and murdered a brother called Pew.

Nothing seemed to hinder the believers of Katin. They continued visiting neighboring villages to share the gospel. So authorities rounded up what had become 80 men, women, and children. They held the believers captive in a school and refused to give them food or water until they signed documents saying they would stop worshipping Jesus. From then on, the families worshipped in small home groups. Seven more families of Katin decided to follow the way of Christ, with the group now numbering more than one hundred.

One day authorities arrived with machine guns and forced the Christians of Katin to march out of their village. As they walked away from the only place they had ever lived, they watched their homes go up in flames. Taken far away to a barren and desolate area, they were left to die. Yet they created a makeshift village of simple huts and planted crops out of season. Amazingly, the crops grew. Just as the harvest was about to be gathered, authorities came and drained the water from their rice fields, then destroyed the crops. They also tore down the fences surrounding the fields so that wild animals could freely eat whatever rice remained.

God continued to provide for these rugged believers. Katin believers had taken the gospel to other villages. Now the people of those villages brought food to them. Carrying on their backs food, seed, and animals, God inspired those who were given the good news to support those who had labored to bring them the gospel. Authorities in that area of Laos gave up their efforts in using famine for forcing faith to fade away.

True nourishment for life comes not from food alone but from God.[23] How well-fed is your soul? What changes would be required to honestly say that you would rather have spiritual nourishment than food? Will you pray for Christ followers deprived of food?

*

---

[23] Matthew 4:4

Nakedness

Γυμνότης gumnotés

bodily exposure

stripped of clothing

Jesus was stripped naked and whipped. He was clothed with the mockery of a King's purple robe while He journeyed to the place of execution. There, he was stripped again and nailed to a cross. Jesus suffered the public humiliation of slow death while naked.[24] Modern portrayals of His death have graciously given Christ a loincloth.

During the decades following Jesus' crucifixion, the Roman empire humiliated Christ followers in just the same way; nailing them naked to crosses on every road leading to Rome. They were also stripped naked before being tossed to wild beasts for entertainment in the coliseum.

Down through the centuries, the forced public stripping of Christians has continued. Many Christ followers have suffered such humiliating abuse. Bodily exposure as a form of persecution against Christians is still common today.

On May 26, 2016, armed Muslims formed a mob. They looted and torched seven Christian homes south of the capitol of Egypt. In the last home, a seventy-year-old grandmother sat stunned as they stripped her. The mob of eighteen men paraded her naked on the streets. Her crime? She allowed her Christ following son to date a Muslim woman and attempt to lead her to convert.

Charles Spurgeon describes the humiliation of Christians through the centuries by forced bodily exposure. He says that while Christians stood naked, the beastly men

---

[24] Matthew 27:28,35.

who tortured them gazed on them with cruel eyes. Yet to Christ-followers at the scene, the bodies of those being humiliated seemed to blaze with holy glory. Those stripped of their clothing looked on their tormentors with calm countenance.[25] Attempts to humiliate Christ's followers through nakedness have only resulted in their glory and the revealing of the embarrassing ugliness of those opposing Christ.

You are either clothed in the shame of your sin, as were Adam and Eve,[26] or you are clothed with Christ[27]. How does God see you?

How would you feel if you were paraded through the streets naked for all to see? Was God the Father embarrassed by the nakedness of God the Son on the cross?

*

Peril

Κίνδυνος *kindunos*

arranged danger
intentional harm

Cheryl and I were blessed with being able to serve more than a decade in Korea assisting the Korean church in developing as a mission-sending base, and nearly a decade focused on evangelism and training Mandarin speaking trainers. There we found ourselves on the front lines of spiritual warfare where light is pushing back darkness. What exactly led to

---

[25] Spurgeon's Sermons Volume 13: 1867 By Charles Haddon Spurgeon
[26] Genesis 2-3
[27] Galatians 3:26-27, Romans 13:14

the government feeling the need to kick our family out of that country? For the answer, let's back up a bit.

Simeon Park was one of my students at the seminary in Korea. I assisted student groups wanting to go on short-term international mission trips. Simeon went with a group to show the Jesus film in the villages of a mountainous demilitarized zone. The team was taken into custody overnight. That didn't stop Simeon from later following our family to leave Korea and move to communist East Asia for the sake of the gospel.

Working with two Singaporean young ladies who felt led to join our team, the three boldly shared Christ with all the new friends they could make in our target city. Within a year, there were new groups of Christ followers meeting in a bowling alley, a floating restaurant, a jewelry shop, a High school, a government office, a city park, and dozens of homes. Jesus became the talk of the town. This was the beginning of the end of our time serving in that part of the country.

Some people were not at all happy about the Jesus invasion in our target city. Shortly after calling me to say he was being followed, Simeon disappeared. I tried calling his number, but a strange man answered saying that Simeon had gone on a trip. In fact, he had been taken for interrogation.

Authorities deprived Simeon of sleep and food. He was beaten and psychologically tortured. They put him on a rack that slowly pulled his body in two different directions, to the left side and to the right. Still he would not give up the names of his co-workers or his computer password.

Neither would he promise to stop telling people about Jesus.

Finally, they induced a drug commonly called "truth serum," and Simeon began to talk. Without any trial, they told Simeon he would spend eight years in prison for spreading spiritual pollution. Had the Korean media not threatened to make an international story out of Simeon's mistreatment, Simeon Park might have died in prison.

By this time, our security crisis -mentioned earlier- forced me out of the country and required that Cheryl and the boys stayed in country. A few days after Simeon's unexpected release and return to Korea I met with Simeon. We wept together for the longest time, with no words being necessary. We were brothers who had survived conflict together. Simeon had suffered far more for Christ than I had.

The enemy doesn't really mess with those who don't risk their lives for Christ. Yet he seeks to intentionally harm those who are dangerous for Jesus. The arranged peril that Simeon faced boldly for Christ caused his own father to turn to faith in Christ, after decades of following Buddhism and Animism.

Recently on a reunion trip to Korea, I was blessed to see how God had given Simeon a lovely wife who spent two years as a single missionary in India. The Parks now have two beautiful children. I had the joy of taking the family on a shopping spree just to bless them. The truth is they blessed me more than I can describe. Simeon not only survived being captured, he is thriving as a pastor of a mission-minded church.

How dangerous does the enemy consider you to be? In what ways should you be more dangerous? Has the enemy ever placed intended harm in your path as you obey Christ?

*

Sword

Μάχαιρα machaira

a staging dagger
a slaughter-knife

For Christ's sake, we His sheep are being led to slaughter all day long. Since the time of Christ, there have been an estimated 70 million of us Christ followers who have died for our faith. More than half of the 70 million of us died in the last 122 years. The number of martyrs for Christ from 1900 until now is greater than those who died for Christ from 33 AD to 1899 AD. Most martyrs since 1900 have been killed by dictators, communist regimes, or terrorists. Some were put to death by their own families and communities.[28]

Syd was my wife Cheryl's good friend and swimming partner during seminary. We often enjoyed having Syd in our home in Dallas. After graduation, Cheryl and I left the U.S. to serve in East Asia. Syd Mizell felt clearly God calling her to Afghanistan as a single lady.

---

[28] https://www.gordonconwell.edu/blog/christian-martyrdom-who-why-how/

She learned the language, lived among the people, and wore a burqa covering herself from head to toe. Syd helped women and families learn how to make things with their hands and have income.

On January 26, 2008, Syd and Hadi, her male co-worker and driver, were abducted by unidentified gunmen in the city of Kandahar, Afghanistan. Later the organization she worked for received information concerning Syd's death. [29]

Syd's parents had talked with her prior to abduction. She told them the local people loved her and cared for her, and that she was respected by the people. Syd Mizell became a martyr at age fifty. As an Afghan martyr, Hadi left behind a wife and five children. Twenty-three South Korean Christians working in Afghanistan were also abducted and most were never found.

Syd was killed in hopes that her death would separate Afghans from the Christ whom Syd taught them to follow. Instead, the love for Syd and the Christ she followed motivated more than 500 women to publically gather in a wedding hall. They risked their own lives to hold a media event stating to the world that Syd had brought God's love to them in Jesus Christ.

These ladies were bold converts from Islam. No doubt some of them have given their lives for Christ. The sword turns martyrs into more than conquerors. A conqueror would have to fight to win. For Christ followers, His love does the fighting for us. His death conquered sin for us. If to live is Christ, then to die is gain.

[29]http://www.cnn.com/2008/WORLD/asiapcf/02/27/afghanistan/index.html
[30] There is still not even one legal evangelical church in Afghanistan. Each of the 20,000 Afghan Christ followers has chosen Christ despite losing all rights as an Afghan citizen.

If God were to call you to Afghanistan, would you go? [30]

If you were an Afghan Christ follower, would you be able to say, "I want to know Christ and experience the mighty power that raised him from the dead. I want to suffer with him, sharing in his death?" (Philippians 3:10)

What would it take to agree that to die is gain? (Philippians 1:21)

*

God's love has been proven over and over again. His love is powerfully personal when we suffer for Christ's sake. Suffering for Christ is to be expected on the mission fields of the world. When returning from twenty years in East Asia, we were surprised by our suffering here in the United Sates while attempting to turn around declining churches.

The enemy obviously wants casual Christians to remain lukewarm and he desires dying churches to keep slowly fading away. It's time for us to become dangerous to the enemy right here in what is now a post- Christian country.

Whether here or there, when we become weak through suffering for Jesus' sake, our victory is our Father's strong love. He carries us through the valley of the shadow of death. Suffering leads to the death of self, which leads to being resurrected with Christ and entering into the joy of becoming fully alive.

So now I live with the confidence

that there is nothing in the universe

with the power to separate us from God's love.

I'm convinced that his love will triumph over

death,

life's troubles,

fallen angels,

or dark rulers in the heavens.

There is nothing in our present or future circumstances that

can weaken his love. There is

no power above us

or beneath us—

no power that could ever be found in the universe

that can distance us from God's passionate love,

which is lavished upon us

through our Lord Jesus, the Anointed One!

Romans 8:38-39 TPT

Love That Won't Let Me Go!

Ever felt like you've been spending a lifetime looking for love in all the wrong places? Even the most passionate erotic love fades over time and fails to make you fully alive. Familial love leaves when your family passes away or when relatives choose to distance themselves from you. The filial love of companions you thought were best friends often disappoints.

All the loves this world can give you can be taken from you. Love is so easily separated from you. To reduce the possibility of further pain that more loss brings, you may find yourself slowly detaching emotionally. Life so easily diminishes to mere existence.

Maybe you feel that the God who created you is distant and that His love for you depends on your performance. You may think you have to *earn* your wings to fly to Him when this life is over.

Finally, thinking there is no love to be given you, you may turn to others for advice about your loveless condition. They might tell you the greatest love of all is learning to love yourself. So you give it a try. At first, you feel the thrill of instant gratification. Over time however, the thrill of self-love turns to frustration.

In the end, you may realize that true love can only be experienced when it is given to you by Someone else. You might be ready to give up on Love ever finding you. Perhaps you are settling for mere existence.

Loveless existence is *not* life. Give me your full attention please. *There* **is** *a love that will not disappoint.* The Creator God fashioned you for the purpose of enjoying a love relationship with Him. His love is not based on feelings. God's love is a commitment to care for His children unconditionally. His love is deeply rooted in His unwavering heart of faithfulness to those who have become His through Christ.

Find Unfailing Love by Falling for Jesus

Nothing ... will ever be able to separate us

from the love of God

that is *revealed in Christ* Jesus our Lord.

Romans 8:39

While every person is God's *creation*, only those who come to God the Father through faith in Jesus as God the Son become God's *children*. If you want to become fully alive by experiencing real love beyond what any human can give you, give your all to Jesus. Ask God to make Himself real to you through the person of Christ Jesus. Get to know Jesus. Let the Lord get to know *you*. Let Him love you. Your Creator waits eagerly to love you.

The moment you surrender your self-sufficiency to Christ's sovereignty is the moment you enter into the Father's ἀγάπη agape love. You've been loveless for too long. Find unfailing love by falling for Jesus. Whatever choosing to follow Christ may cost you, His love is more than worth it.

If you have fallen in love with Christ, you are becoming fully alive. His love is inseparable from you. Through it all, you're learning to *trust in Jesus as He unleashes more and more of your Father's love into your heart.* Christ is always in you, bringing you unbeatable victory.

Christ's love within you makes you always favored by your Father. He will never get tired of you. God will never give up on you. His ἀγάπη agape love commits Him to care unconditionally for you, though you are frail, imperfect, and sometimes rebellious. The Father's

> *Trust in Jesus as He unleashes more and more of your Father's love into your heart.*

love is truly a love that just will not *ever* let you go.

Jesus will never tell you He's done with your relationship. With Christ in you, you are becoming *unstoppable* because His love is *inseparable*.

My friend, can you utter such conviction as true for you? If you are not sure, I must ask you this question. Have you found unfailing love by falling for Jesus?

Face Death Fearlessly Through His Love

Nothing can ever separate us from God's love.

Neither *death*…

Romans 8:38

As a hospice chaplain, I have seen repeatedly that death can be a terrible ordeal. Many of my patients become like family to me. Sometimes the slow agony and constant pain day after day feels like it's just too much. The death process can be extremely difficult, perhaps more difficult than any other experience. Yet even so, if you belong to Jesus, He is with you all the way through the dying process.

If you have fallen for Jesus as the Love of your life, death cannot and will not separate you from God's love. You need not, and should not, fear death. Through the suffering death brings, His love becomes even stronger.

At the moment your physical body ceases to function and you depart from this earth, the real you will ascend to be with the Lord. In that instant your spirit will travel from your body to the Lord. He will do the transporting of your soul. *You will be carried into eternity on His wings of love.* Those wings are given only by accepting God's underserved favor through faith in Christ. You cannot earn your wings to fly to heaven.[31]

John Bruce was a federal judge appointed by Ulysses S. Grant. On his death bed, he turned to his daughter.

He softly said, "Fetch the book. Turn to Romans eight. Put my finger on 'Neither death nor life...'"

She found those words, and put his finger on them. He passed away with his finger on the promise that death cannot separate the Christ follower from God's love. John Bruce traveled into eternity without any fear on the face he left behind.

Find unfailing love by falling for Jesus. Face death fearlessly through His love. Fetch the book and put your finger on His promise. Anchor your soul there.

Shed Insecurity Through His Inseparable Love

Nothing can ever separate us

from God's love.

Neither death *nor life*...

Romans 8:38

Without Christ, you can't help but feel insecure in this crazy world. You may ask yourself, "Who am I? Where do I fit in? Where is my place in this world?"

You won't find your place in this world until you find Christ. Find Him, and you can become secure in God's love. Christ is your hiding place of security in this dangerous world.

---

[31] See Romans 3:23, 6:23, and Ephesians 2:8-10

Insecurity focuses on who you are. Security in Christ focuses on *Whose* you are. Insecurity looks at life and freaks out in fear. Security looks at Christ and falls into His arms.

If you are in Christ, your distresses and suffering just make His love *exert* itself even more evidently and clearly. Through life's trying experiences, you don't hold on to God. He holds on to you! You can go through anything with a sense of settled security because His love is going with you.

Neither the trials or the thrills of your life can pull you away from God's attachment to you. The trials drive you to dependence on the Divine. The occasional thrill of life may make you start to chill about God, so He turns up the heat to remind you that it's *His grace and love* that brings life's true thrills.

> *Insecurity focuses on who you are. Security focuses on Whose you are.*

Life and death are bookends showcasing the volumes of God's works of love.

- Volume one shows how He loves you before your life began.
- Volume two tells of how He chases after you.
- In volume three, He causes you to be born a second time, as you start to become spiritually alive.
- Though you wobble like a toddler, in volume four His hand comes and steadies you as a newborn child of God in Christ.
- Volume five reveals God's love leading you triumphantly through all of life's experiences.

- Volume six shows how your own fickle faith doesn't cause the flame of His love to flicker.
- The seventh volume is written in invisible ink yet to be revealed, because it is not yet clear just how and when His love will carry you into glory.

Stop to read these volumes of His love for you.

We live among those who doubt God cares, or that He has the power to change this messed-up world. It could be that right now you doubt His Divine doings. Listen. God still has you in His grasp. You may have considered leaving Him. He never leaves you. Even if you do attempt to forsake Him, the Lord God will never forsake you.

Inside God's love, you have a safe zone, a place you can relax without the fear of not being fully accepted. In His love, you can let down your guard. Experiencing His love causes you to confide in your Father's safety. His love moves you to trust Him with your whole self. Shed that pre-Christ insecurity. Live with the security of experiencing the depths of His inseparable love.

> Trust your whole self to His love.

Here's my challenge to you. Spend time with the Father. Time with Him helps a sense of security grow within you. Listen closely, and His voice will remind you of His love.

Practice daily verbalizing the inseparable presence of His love, and you will become secure. Here's a bit of Christ-centered Tai Chi. While moving your body, arms, and hands to match the words, say, "God, you've got my back. You are in front of me. You are on my left and you are on my right. Lord, you are above me and below me. You are within me. You surround me with your love.

Your love exudes from within me. I am fully loved and forever accepted by you. I'm secure in Christ."

Let life just go on and rain down misery on you. It's all water rolling off the duck's back. Keep on paddling your way across the pond. Better yet, use those wings he's given you to fly. Soar high for God's glory. Shine in whatever way God says shine during the days He gives you. The shine doesn't show who *you* are. It shows *Whose* you are. Shed insecurity because His love is inseparable. Anchor your soul in the certainty of His love.

Despite Paranormal Activity Around You, Be Quieted by His Love Within You

Nothing can ever separate us

from God's love.

Neither ... angels nor demons

Romans 8:38

Why are angels even mentioned? Surely they would never come between you and God. Aren't angels 100% angelic all of the time? Actually, though it is very unusual, God's angels have been known to wander away from Him and lead others astray.[32]

As a general rule, guardian angels are great, but they are not capable of omnipresence. They are separable from you. They may leave you to go help someone who needs their help more than you.

---

[32] See Ezekiel 28:12-17, Isaiah 14:12-15, Luke 10:18, Revelation 12:4

Thank God for the help of angels but lean solely on the One whose love is inseparable. Unlike angels, He never ever leaves you. His love is more beautiful than an angel. His care for you is more angelic than all the angels combined.

In our scientific society, we label most every paranormal behavior with medical terms such as "syndrome." We give paranormal activity scientific explanations, describing them as "invisible energy fields." We tend to explain away unseen spiritual phenomena.

Beware my friend. When you are glowing with God's glorious grace and when you are unbeatable through the security of His inseparable love, the enemy will not rest. In the unseen realm where he does his dirty work, Satan's demons will seek to bring you down by troubling your soul.

Just as angels are real and powerful, so are demons. One of the enemy's dirtiest tricks is deceiving modern people into thinking demons are only for superstitious uneducated people.

Demons have power to …

… depress your mind,

… detour your direction,

.. deteriorate your flesh, and

… destroy the soul.

Is Christ in you? Greater is He who is in you than he who is in this world.

No matter how numerous, scary and pesky Satan's varmints may be, they cannot spook away God's love.

Those little rascals certainly don't scare your big God. Instead, Christ's power in you spooks demons terribly!

The unseen spiritual realm around you is more real than the visible material world. Be aware of spiritual activity. Learn to discern the spirits. Do not be troubled by them or take much interest in them. Despite paranormal activity around you, be quieted by His love within you.

Live as Though Whatever Happens Pulls Him Closer

Nothing can ever separate us

from God's love.

Neither our *fears for today*…

Romans 8:38

What do you fear today? Failing health? Financial difficulties? A possible relational break-up? Following Christ does not keep bad things from happening. But when bad things happen to you as a Christ follower, they don't make Him love you less. Tough times draw Him even nearer.

No predicament can pull Him away from you.

No turmoil can push His love out of your heart.

No crisis of faith will cause Him to give up on you.

No temptation you face makes Him leave you.

No persistent sin separates you from His love.

No pain takes away His presence.

No bitter grief gets God to go away.

The fears of today may distress you. They do not, however, remove God's love from you. They all bring God's love even closer to you. Live as though whatever happens pulls His love closer, because it does!

Receive the Future as Gift-wrapped from Him

Nothing can ever separate us

from God's love.

Neither our fears for today

nor our worries about tomorrow…

Romans 8:38

You are no doubt concerned about things to come. Who will you marry? How will your life turn out? What will you be like at middle age? Who will care for you when you are old? What will become of your children and grandchildren? None of us can see the future through a crystal ball.

On my way to the athletic club to swim, I pass by a sign in front of an old house left standing in what is now a business district. The sign says, "Palm Reader: Discover Your Future Here." One day I decided to write an email to the one who works there.

Dear Spiritist,

Not so long ago, I received a love letter that told me my future. The letter told me of a great love that had been saved up for me for some time. I had previously not known this lover before reading the letter. Though I doubted the sincerity of the writer's love for me, soon the lover made clear that this love was deeper than any love I had known before. I said "yes" to the offer of love.

Now this new love of mine has made certain my future, so I regret to inform you that I have no need of your services. I do however, want to make you aware that I am now empowered to predict your future. I offer this service to you free of charge, although it may cost your life.

Here is an app with the same love letter written to you as well. https://www.bible.com/

Without this love, your future is bleak. If you say yes to this love, your future is out of this world. This love even helps people break away from spiritual alignments like the one you seem to have fallen into.

Kept by Unbreakable Love[33]

Worried about things to come? God's love has kept up with you in your past and will be with you into your future. You don't need a palm reader.

If you are in Christ, He has told you your future. Use your voice to remind yourself of His promises.

God, I know you will go on loving me. You will keep pouring into me the entire fullness of Your life and Your glory. Whatever my difficulties, I will gain by my losses, succeed by my failures, and triumph through my defeats. Your love has destined me to glory. In Your love, my future is to become more than a conqueror. Nothing can ever separate me from Your love. Through Your love in me, I am becoming fully alive.

Receive whatever your future brings you as a love-gift wrapped by God.

---

[33] The letter was never sent. No need to initiate dialogue with the dark side. If you are under attack, call on the Lord Jesus to take on the enemy.

Fearlessly Encounter any Power on Earth

For I am persuaded that not even ... hostile powers ...

will have the power to separate us

from the love of God ...in Christ Jesus our Lord!

Romans 8:38-39 HCSB

There are many great powers on this earth. The power of drugs keeps many people addicted, destroying lives, families, communities, and nations. Powerful strongholds of the mind keep alive much deceitful stinkin' thinkin.' The North Korean dictator keeps an entire population brainlessly following him, despite death from malnutrition.

Perhaps powers at work in your own life make you feel unable to change. The lure of a stubborn sin lingers on. A relationship problem which should have been dealt with long ago still oppresses you.

> *If there were* a power that could separate you from God's love, that would be the greatest power ever. *There is no such power.*

The power of people who do wrong seems to overcome the good you want to see happen. Progressive "Christianity" attacks the Bible, seeking to convince people that there's no power in the blood of Christ alone to save mankind from sin.

Hostile power encounters can seem bigger than life, and can make us feel those powers are bigger than God's power. Yet God's love overpowers all powers. No power can propel His love away from you.

If there were a power that could separate you from God's love, that would be the greatest power ever. *There is no such power.* The love of God is simply the greatest power there is. His love overpowers all.

If all this is true, why does it sometimes not *seem* to be true? Because God's power is not that of a forceful dictator. He does not program robots to serve Him mindlessly. Instead, He gives those He created freedom to choose to live within the blessings of His Kingdom power, or to be subjects to the hostile powers of the world's dark kingdom.

If you have chosen the power of life in Christ, His resurrection power has invaded your soul. During that invasion, the former hostile dictator was dethroned from being king of your heart, and a wonderful benevolent Ruler has taken the throne. Christ is now your King. He is taking you from mere mortal existence into the process of immortalization. He is making you fully and eternally alive.

The invasion of the Spirit into your being has created a disruption causing hostile powers to no longer be at home in you. Those enemies may still pester you from a distance, but now Christ possesses you. The minions of Satan may throw tantrums because you are no longer possessed by *them.*

There is simply nothing they can do to undo your adoption. You have become a kid of the King of Kings and Lord of Lords. As an eternal Kingdom Kid, all the King's love is yours now and forever. He is yours and you are His.

There's a bond between you and the Lord that no power can break, not now, not ever.

You may still bump into dark places in this world. Along your life's journey you will no doubt arrive at destinations where the light of Christ is unknown. You may sense the workings of evil here and there, and sometimes everywhere. You will occasionally choose sin, only to regret having done so. Through the power of God's inseparable love, may you fearlessly encounter and overcome the powers of this earth.

Explore Every Space without Fear

No power *in the sky above*

or in the earth below—

will ever be able to separate us

from the love of God ... in Christ Jesus our Lord.

Romans 8:39

Just as no power can propel His love from you, no *place* can put any space between you and His love. You may be put in a place of high honor, yet His love goes with you there as you honor Him. You may be taken to a deep place through a disgraceful decision. Even there, He disciplines you and abides with you in love.

Measuring from the earth's center, the tallest place in the world is the peak of Mount Everest, between Nepal and Tibet. So go on. Get your portable oxygen ready, and join the few hundred people per year attempting to climb 29,032 feet to the summit. His majestic love goes with you as you discover He is the air you breathe.

The deepest point on the planet is near Guam, six miles under water. If technology were developed to do so, you could travel through tremendously crushing water pressure to that deepest point on the earth's floor. His love would already be there with you. Even at that depth, the Lord's love would neither be crushed nor crush you.

If you were to look through the most modern telescope into outer space it would be but a peephole view into God's infinite love. You can travel through zero gravity in space and God's love doesn't float away. You can venture down to the ocean depths of pressures more than one thousand times that of our atmosphere, and God's love could stand the pressure and stay with you.

Even if you could escape the limits of the space defining our universe and the limits of time defining our lives, God's love would not escape you. He and His love are unlimited by space and time. He is boundless immortality. You may feel like a mere mortal now, but His love is preparing you for immortality with Him. Life on earth in Christ's love makes us mystically uncomfortable in the now as we transition toward our real home real soon.

He is everywhere, and so is His love. So go on now and explore without fear every place God takes you. His love is inescapable.

Enjoy His Protection in His Arms of Love

Neither …height, nor depth,

nor any other creature,

shall be able to separate us from the love of God…

Romans 8:39 ASV

As Paul wrote to believers in Rome, the Emperor Nero was turning himself into almost everyone's hero. He provided for the modern citizens of the Roman Empire luxuries not previously known. They enjoyed indoor plumbing, air conditioned homes, luscious gardens, and ample entertainment. The citizens applauded Nero as the god of good use of their tax dollars.

Then along came some who dared to be politically incorrect by refusing to agree that the Roman Caesar was Lord. Instead, they said that some *dead* person named Jesus was Lord. The people of Rome were embarrassed by such supposed barbarians. So Nero came to the rescue. He declared that he would rid the Roman Empire of the "Jesus is Lord" people.

He placed Jesus lovers on crosses hanging at every entrance into Rome. He rolled believers in tar and lit them for night lights in his garden. He threw believers into the famed coliseum and then unleashed wild animals into the arena. He even burned Rome and blamed it on the Christians.

Those who first read Romans eight were heavily persecuted for following Christ. Today, persecution may come to you as well. Nero wants your allegiance, and if he doesn't get it, he may send creatures out to devour you. Nero is not your hero. Your Beloved is your hero.

The lion, the tiger, the beast, the dragon[34], and the Nero of our world may all gang up against you. They may pull you apart, but they cannot pull the Father's love away from you. He always stands with you. Regardless of what the world's creatures may do to your flesh, the Lord's love is always protecting your soul. He tames every creature before it can reach the real you. Enjoy protection in the arms of His love.

His love is more intoxicating than any brew. The Lord's love is more invigorating than Minnesota winter air. His love is more calming than a Korean sauna. God's love is fresher than spring in the Kunming mountains.

His love is softer than a baby's bottom. The Father's love revives the heart better than CPR. His love triumphs better than a Trojan horse.

At some point, like Paul, you may run out of analogies and that's when God's love has only just begun to make you fully alive.

---

[34] See Revelation 12-13.

Discussion Questions

1. Read Romans 8:38-39 in the Message Paraphrase and two other translations. Write and then vocalize your own prayer speaking directly to God, describing His love for you. Your prayer should touch on every Biblical idea.

   "God Your love for me is….

2. Ever found yourself looking for love in all the wrong places? How did that work out?

3. What is one of your favorite things about God's love, as described in Romans 8:38-39?

4. Read I Corinthians 13 in The Message Paraphrase. Note the practical outcomes in your life which will

be present when God's love is flowing into you and spilling over into your relationships with others:

-
-
-
-
-
-
-
-

5. What is God saying to you through this chapter?

The Persuaded Life

Some people say, "You are what you eat." We had a friend who was certain she needed to lose weight. Though it appeared to us that her weight was already just right, she ate nothing but carrots day after day. Her skin actually began to turn as orange as a carrot! Does your life revolve around your appearance?

We often hear the advice, "Follow your heart. Do what's best for *you*." This life mantra suggests you go with your own feelings, instinct, or inclination. Do you live by your own impressions?

Other people say, "Let your conscience be your guide. Each of us are to do what is right in our own eyes." What's right for me could be wrong for you, and vice versa. If it is right in your own eyes, you might convince yourself than you can literally get away with murdering someone. As they say in Tennessee, "Now, that just ain't right."

Let's one up it, shall we? Instead of letting your conscience be your guide, *let your convictions be your guide*. You *are* your core convictions. The future you is being formed right now by whatever inner persuasions you hold on to most passionately.

What on earth are you here for? On what foundation do your base your decisions? What constitutes your core being? Why do you think the way you think and act the way you act? What are your convictions?

If you don't know what your convictions are, you don't really know *who* you are. You may know your name, family history, abilities, personal likes and dislikes. But until you know what you would die for, you don't know what you are living for.

We are not talking about mere beliefs. A child has been told that fire burns. She *believes* what her parents say is true. She has also seen that marshmallows burn when put in the fire. She believes.

Yet how can she know for sure about fire? One day when no one is looking, she places her hand in the fire. In that moment of personal experience, she has moved *from believing to knowing*.

Prior to experience, there is belief. After experience, there is persuasion. Being taught a thing may result in belief in it, but it doesn't necessarily persuade the heart to *live* by that belief. Experience persuades. Experienced-based persuasion is conviction.

> Let experiencing God move you from believing to knowing.

You've been taught by the fiery Spirit of God. And if you have read this far in the book, you no doubt believe in Jesus. Yet have you experienced the touch of the Spirit's flame purifying your life? Are you regularly experiencing God's mystical presence, love, and discipline? Through personally experiencing God, do you find that your life is becoming centered more and more around settled convictions based on His truth?

Romans eight gives us the challenge to *live by convictions from the Spirit*. In this volume, you have journeyed together with me all the way through chapter eight of Romans, going in-depth into each and every phrase. I've enjoyed our time together, as I trust you have as well.

> Live by convictions from the Spirit.

It's like we've each picked up an apple and ate around that apple in sync with each other. We have eaten all we could at the depth of one bite into each part of the apple. We see that what is left of our apple is the core.

The core of Romans eight is conviction. *When the core of who you are is shaped by experienced-based Spirit-produced convictions, then you are becoming fully alive.* Your deepest convictions define your character, your behavior, and your life's direction.

Convictions are lessons learned while life happens to you. You may never want to go through those experiences again, but you wouldn't trade them for anything. They shape your life. Convictions are taught by some of the toughest teachers, like failure, loss, disappointment and agony.

I am convinced…

Romans 8:38

The word "convince" πέπεισμαι (*pepeismai*) literally means "to bind." Think Velcro with superglue. *Pepesmai* is the perfect tense of the root word *pistos*, or faith. A conviction is faith in a particular truth from God that perfectly and permanently binds itself to your heart.

The Spirit uses your life experiences to create and solidify the conviction deep within your core.

To be convinced is to become permanently bound to a particular conviction based on experience. A conviction comes from being induced by experience to live by a particular truth.

To become convinced or persuaded, you must first allow God to lead you through an experience which causes you to become certain of something within your mind. Are you willing to allow God to lead you into situations you might not have otherwise chosen? Can you sincerely say to Him, "Wherever You lead, I'll go"?

> When who you are is shaped by experienced-based, Spirit-produced convictions, then you are becoming fully alive.

Though I would have chosen to spend my first university summer working full-time at KROK as a DJ, God made it clear I was to go on summer missions. During that summer of 1981 in Washington and Idaho, I was asked to teach children the Bible, lead Sunday morning worship, and share the message of Christ door to door. I had never done any of that before.

I said yes, and through the convictions which emerged, the trajectory of my life changed radically. As a nineteen-year-old, my heart changed from continuing as a rock and roll disc jockey to serving God with all He has entrusted to me.

Radically following God with 100% obedience brings experiences that mold convictions. God's truth, bound to your heart through past experience, begins to change your future behavior. To be persuaded is to be so confident about your convictions that you stake your life on them, regardless of the consequences.

Cheryl and I have held to our convictions in pressurized situations, and as a result, repeatedly suffered greatly. God's Spirit blessed us in unexplainable ways during such suffering. To compromise conviction is to suffocate the life-giving Spirit of God within. To stand on conviction is to be fully alive through the Spirit.

> Your deepest convictions define you.

In the chapters of *Becoming Fully Alive*, we have zoomed in closely and examined every truth carefully. We now zoom out, looking at the big picture of Romans eight. As we do so, may the Spirit catalyze and clarify core convictions by which He helps us in becoming fully alive day by day.

For my own personal walk with God, I have written my own response to Romans chapter eight. This declaration of who I am assists me in *living out* what the Spirit is *working in* to my life.

I am Fully Alive in the Spirit

God, through dependence on Your Spirit in me, I am daily becoming fully alive. Through experiencing You in my day to day life, I have these core convictions:

I am *free*. **I live by Your Spirit's freedom.**

- I am free from feeling condemned. (8:1)
- I am free from the control of sin. (8:2-3,5)
- I am free because You are satisfied with me. (8:4)
- I am free to be fully alive in Your Spirit. (8:6-10)

I am *empowered*. **I live in the power of Your Spirit.**

- I live by the power of the blood over my sin. (8:4)
- I live set apart for You by the Spirit's power. (8:11-14)
- I live as the King's power-endued kid. (8:15-17)

I am *eager*. **I live looking forward toward Your presence.**

- I am ready for You to give me a large inheritance. (8:17)
- I am waiting for You to fit me with a heavenly body. (8:11,17)
- I am yearning for You to replace my suffering with glory. (8:18-25)

I am *God-confident*. **I live victoriously through Your Spirit.**

- My prayers in the Spirit are effective. (8:26-27)
- My Spirit-produced outcomes are good. (8:28-30)
- My suffering makes me a Spirit-inspired overcomer. (8:31-37)
- My love life with You is unbreakable. (8:38-39)

Based on Romans eight, what convictions are God reinforcing at your core? Consider writing your own statement of convictions. You can use my statement above for starter thoughts, or write your own from scratch.

- ✓ Write and say your convictions to yourself regularly, looking in the mirror. When you speak God's truth about yourself to yourself, you will be moved by the emotions that come up from within. Those emotions are the Spirit super-naturalizing your personality.
- ✓ Share the declaration of your convictions with a few trusted friends. You will be blessed by their encouragement and by your contagiousness in Christ.
- ✓ Visualize how the truths God is showing you are changing the trajectory of your life. Your experiences with God bind convictions to your heart with deep persuasion.

Let's take one last look at Romans eight. God desires to use your life experiences to mold convictions within you. I conclude by mentioning some experiences God used in my own life to shape who I am becoming. May my examples given here prompt a God-inspired continuing quest within you toward becoming fully alive in the Spirit.

I Live Free

I have no dark cloud of condemnation hanging over me. (8:1) There is no slavery to sin. (8:2-3,5) Exhilarating freedom is mine through knowing that God is satisfied with me in Christ. (8:4) So, I am free to live fully alive in the Spirit. (8:6-10)

Over the decades of ministry, efforts to condemn me have been many. Some attempts to bring me down came from professional jealousy. Condemnation tried to grab ahold of my heart through slander, and through attacks on our family. Sometimes condemning voices came from within myself. My own sin would try to haunt me.

Had I let those dark condemning clouds linger above me, the enemy would have lured me away from what Christ had for me. To consistently stay clear of feeling condemned, I must remind myself regularly of what God says is true about me. I must also spend time with friends who hold these same convictions of truth.

With the Spirit giving us freedom to be fully alive, Cheryl and I have been blessed to experience four decades of journeying into whatever new horizon the Lord has next for us. From church planting in Texas, missionary training in Korea, mass seed sowing in the Mandarin speaking world, or seeking to revitalize declining churches in the U.S., we have been free to let the Spirit wind blow as He will.

What experienced-based persuasions has the Lord given you concerning your freedom in the Spirit, based on Romans 8:1-10? How have you seen these convictions tested through life's trials? What specific freedoms has the Spirit given you? In what ways do you desire more freedom in the Spirit?

I Live Empowered

Jesus' blood shed for me on the cross has powerfully washed away my sin. (8:4) God's grip of love on my heart gives me a powerful passion to live holy, set a part for God. (8:11-14) I have been permanently adopted as God's empowered child. (8:15-17)

After spending the summer of 1981 serving God in Washington State, I was challenged by First Baptist Church of Ore City, Texas to start a worship gathering in a small community on Lake O' the Pines where there was no congregation. I was a nineteen-year-old rock 'n roll disc jockey.

I had no clue what I was doing. So I just depended on God to lead us. He provided a place for us to worship on Sundays. It was a bait store called Pop's Landing. South Side Church had more than 50 people inside Pop's Landing on our first Sunday. The next Sunday, a big long bus pulled up, already outfitted to be the church nursery.

Within a few months, a cattle rancher I had never met showed up at the door of the little cabin provided for my use.

"Are you Matthew Nance, pastor of South Side Church?"

"Yes Sir."

"Get in my truck."

Off road we went over dozens of hills along the main road into the community. We rode all the way out to the highway without saying much of anything. Then he stopped.

"God owns the cattle on a thousand hills, and He has entrusted to me all the cattle and hills you've just seen. Which hill would be the best hill for South Side Baptist Church?"

I chose the highest hill on the sharpest curve in the road. The man cut two holes through the fence, laid down drainage pipes and put down gravel for us to meet on our own land the following Sunday!

The men of the church went right to work constructing our first building. God did it all without us even having a plan as to what would happen! With the help of First Church Ore City, we didn't owe a single penny. God stirred the heart of a Godly man to move God's cattle off one of God's hills, making room for a new house of worship. He also orchestrated pastor and people to come together just at the right time with hearts united toward building His church.

Many people placed their faith in Christ while I was pastor of South Side. From that first experience expanding the Kingdom, God seared some convictions deep into my heart.

It's about my availability not my ability. He *empowers those who step out on faith* and depend solely on His ability. He is more than able. When God gives a *vision*, He gives *provision* for the vision. He gives His power to those who seek to build His Kingdom.

What experiences has God brought your way to convict you of His power, and of His empowering? The power is transferred to His children through holy living. Have you come to the place where you think of your life as being set apart for God's purpose? What experiences might God bring into your life to persuade you toward new or renewed convictions from Romans 8:4,11-17?

I Live Forward

One day soon, God will give me an inheritance worth the wait. (8:17) He will transform this frail body into an immortal body. (8:11,17) He will take me from the suffering of this world into the awesome glory of being face to face with Him. (8:18-25)

Living forward means that Cheryl and I travel light through this world. We hold on loosely to things we would otherwise consider as "ours." Time, money, possessions, dwelling places, relationships, investments, influence- all these things are on loan from Him to use in living forward toward His Kingdom.

We live forward by leaning into God. We find He is always several steps ahead of us. God is on the move, and we want to keep in step with Him. If we don't lean into Him, we easily get stuck in the legacy of our past or the challenges of our present.

Living forward requires us to ruthlessly evaluate whether or not our current way of life is still what God wants. Cheryl and I lean into God together. Wherever He has us go in this world to do whatever He has for us to do there, our "go" bag is literally already packed.

So many times we have left all our physical belongings behind to be sold or given away, and have moved to another country taking only two bags each. Sometimes it was by our own sense of God's will. Other times it was forced on us by a hostile government or by circumstances.

Regardless of the situation, each time God has faithfully repositioned us with a new, fresh Kingdom-building challenge. We lean forward eager to know what He wants us to be when we grow up. ⬚ So what's next God?

When you read of the eternal Kingdom to come in Romans 8:17-25, what causes you to marvel? In what ways might God be intentionally having you uncomfortably groan your way through this world, and for what purpose? Through what experiences has God given you what specific convictions about living forward? How might He be nudging you out of your comfort zone?

I Live God Confident

My confidence is based on the Spirit connecting my prayer life to the Father. (8:26-27) Whatever may happen, God works it all out for good. (8:28-30) If I suffer for Christ's sake, it's just God at work turning me into an overcomer. (8:31-37) My greatest security comes from God never removing His love from me. (8:38-39)

Cheryl, myself and our two boys lived in communist East Asia for many years. We personally were persecuted and forced to leave the country. Some of our Asian teammates suffered more than we did.

Before such experiences of really sacrificing for Christ's sake, we didn't fully understand the depth of faith within the believers there. We didn't understand why the number of Christ followers was multiplying in that country more quickly than anywhere in the world.

When a person in a house church there says they want to follow Christ, they are asked a few questions before being baptized.

"If the police come to get you, will you deny you are a Christ follower?"

"If they torture you, will you agree to quit telling people about Jesus?"

"If they take your family, will you turn away from Christ?"

"If they prepare to take your life; what will you do then?"

In that country, giving your life to Christ means just that. To decide to follow Christ is to decide to be counter-cultural, which inevitably creates friction, often brings imprisonment, and sometimes results in death.

Choosing Christ means you are ready to die for Christ. The more the underground church is persecuted, the more Christ followers become persuaded in following Christ to the very end, and the more the flames of Christ's Spirit spread.

Have you decided to be radical in following Christ to go wherever and do whatever He says? Your Christ-centered lifestyle might create friction in our self-centered culture. Your suffering for Christ might cause you to fellowship with Christ in a deeper way than you ever have before.

The pre-Christians around you might become attracted to whatever it is that makes you bold enough to be counter-cultural. You might see God work through you to draw people to Himself. Now *that* would be sharing in His suffering *and* His glory!

> When God's church is lit by the Spirit, persecution just fans the flames.

Are you willing for God to bring persecution into your life? What if your friends make fun of you or unfriend you? What if your boss tells you to leave Jesus at home, or get fired? What if your family labels you a *Jesus Freak*?

May the following be true of you as a core conviction: "I willingly fellowship with Christ in His suffering." Sharing in Christ's glory means sharing in His suffering.

So our journey is complete. Or perhaps it's just begun. We've only just begun to live fully alive in the Spirit!

I pray that you will swim upstream with the Spirit despite the strong current of ungodliness trying to pull you downstream. I pray that any resulting trials that may come as you follow Christ will forge obedience-based convictions made of steel within you. With the Spirit of Christ in you, you are becoming fully alive.

Other Books by Dr. J. Matthew Nance

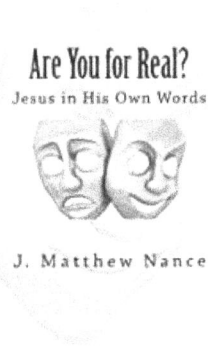

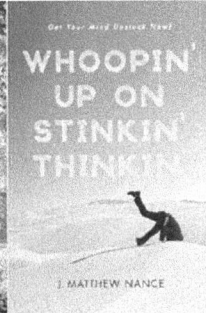